MILLIONS VANISHED

Unveiling Raptures and Resurrections

BRIAN PAUL LAKINS

All Scripture quotations contain the
OLD AND NEW TESTAMENTS
of the
AUTHORIZED OR KING JAMES VERSION TEXT
Always read next to an open Bible (Acts 17:11; 1 Thess. 5:21; 2 Tim. 2:15)

Copyright © 2016 Brian Lakins

All rights reserved. No part of this publication may be reproduced, distributed, or transmitted in any form or by any means, including photocopying, recording, or other electronic or mechanical methods, without the prior written permission of the publisher, except in the case of brief quotations embodied in reviews and certain other non-commercial uses permitted by copyright law.

www.MillionsVanished.com
For more information, please email: *1thes4.16@gmail.com*

Cover Design and Interior Layout & Design by
Quest Publications
(Email: *questpublications@outlook.com*)

Published By:
Quest Publications
6-176 Henry Street
Brantford, ON, N3S 5C8
Canada

Rev. Date: 19-Aug-16

ISBN-13: 978-0-9951872-2-1
ISBN-10: 0-9951872-2-3

DEDICATION

God first, always God first! He wrote the story of His plan for man through the ages. All I've done here is relay the message. The glory is His. I dedicate all to You.

There is absolutely no way I could have accomplished this book or any other if it were not for my wife, Darcie. She lives her life glued to our handsome son, and our beautiful daughter, raising future giants in the kingdom of God and of heaven. I have no doubt that she wishes I would come home from work and save her for only an hour so she can go to the bathroom by herself, but I have been committed to this book, whose research has been studied upon for as long as she has known me. I appreciate her like no other for allowing me the time to write and for sharing her life with mine. All that I am graced to accomplish with her will be greatly rewarded to her account.

A special mention of dedication must be given to Finis Jennings Dake, who is to me how Paul was to Timothy. Though I did not know him in life, I am eternally grateful for his dedication and passion of studying and teaching God's Word. Through the past eight years I have devoured his invaluable notes and references found throughout the Dake Annotated Reference Bible.

CONTENTS

1. Why You Can Believe the Rapture Will Happen..........1
2. Raptures and Resurrections Defined and Understood...9
3. Reasons for The Rapture of the Church and The Tribulation 20
4. Outlining All Resurrections and Raptures....................34
5. Unveiling Resurrections Through Time 41
6. Unveiling Raptures Through Time 79
7. Rapture Qualifications, How To Be Found Worthy ..152
8. The Rapture Motivation 162

APPRECIATION

To my dad, Gary Paul, my mom, Wawanna, sister, Gina, and brother, Craig for surrounding me through life with their godly lives. I wish I could have been a support in their Christian walk, but I was not. Today, I hope to make up for wasted years and help them get closer to God with the wisdom, knowledge, and understanding that comes only through His Word.

I'd like to give a special mention of appreciation for my friend, Brian Morgan, and my cousin, Tracy Silver for helping me with the book cover idea. They happen to both be inspiring people in my life that are authentic in their walk with Christ. Thank you both! Though I am silent with my thoughts, you both have encouraged me greatly in my Christian walk, and I deeply appreciate your willingness to help in any way you could with this book. May the reward from God be great upon you both for ever and ever!

INTRODUCTION

Congratulations! You just picked out an excellent book on the teaching of "the rapture." You won't be disappointed. This is a complex subject made simple. Any and all points of view are consistently supported with numerous Scripture from beginning to end. Your limited time will be well spent and you'll have all the rapture and resurrection references placed in one single source. However, the added pieces that make up God's plan for the human race are all spoken of so that the entire symphony will play out in perfect harmony.

The rapture of the church has been the focus of all rapture teachings for the last two centuries, but the real focus should be on the resurrections. A rapture to immortality is a by-product of the resurrection, yet there are two different resurrections consisting of many raptures. All phases, kinds, and parts of every rapture and resurrection have been laid out through this book to give you a proficient knowledge that will make you the expert.

You will be a master navigator for people who are traveling through the murky waters of 20th and 21st century end-time teachings with all its countless beliefs and fallacies all thrown together. The implications of so many teachings have left the church confused and divided. Tough Christian questions deserve tough biblical answers. You can now be the navigator that helps your circle of influence understand just how important this subject is for their lives, now and forever. Book 2 will even teach you how to address the many timing views of the rapture of the church (pre-tribulation, preterism,

Introduction

partial, pre-wrath, mid-tribulation, post-tribulation, and pan-tribulation).

I encourage you to have a Bible in hand to examine all things (Acts 17:11; 1 Thess. 5:21). Be assured, there has been no new information in this book, but I promise that so many writings here will be new and refreshing to even the most astute and seasoned end-time student and teacher. The unveiling of this information is not a revealing of new information, as if God has given another revelation of His Word. God forbid! The unveiling is that of the eyes and understanding of man, so that the compatibility of all Scripture can be seen (2 Cor. 4:4; 2 Pt. 1:19-21).

Imagine a puzzle of 10,000 pieces with no picture on the box. It would be complicated to understand unless you started to place those pieces together correctly, and then you would start to see the picture. Many teachers and students of Bible prophecy have numerous sections of the puzzle fitted together so that they see some clear images, but they stop short of piecing them all together for the complete picture. The same concept must happen with Scripture.

Now, imagine this: living in a time when millions of people from around the world just vanish without a trace. Would you be one of them? A better question: Would you want to be one of them? If you were left behind, would you understand why this event occurred or where those people went? Do you know what to expect when you are taken or left behind?

Well, this is a reality that many Bible students and teachers believe is an experience that can be expected in our life time. This book will give you a complete understanding of this event most commonly referred to as, the rapture. If you've ever felt claustrophobic in your own skin, like an inner yearning to burst out of your flesh and live what must be the reality a perfect Creator meant for you, an existence with no sin, no pain, no aging, no real physical limitations, then this book is for you! After all, that and so much more is what the rapture promises.

All cultures throughout time and across the many regions of earth have one thing in common, they believed in at least one higher power and they believed there is a future resurrection. Some notorious atheists who carried the torch for their religious orientation, such as Sir Francis Newport, Ethan Allen, Tom Paine, and Voltaire have renounced atheism in times of affliction, even pleading for mercy from God when looking eternity in the eye. God Almighty Himself put that in our DNA and all who are honest with themselves, no matter what their religious views, will acknowledge their own DNA impression and inclination that life is forever. Maybe that impression God placed in all of us is why I always cleaved onto the rapture doctrine from the moment it was first taught to me.

I vaguely recall learning about the rapture in children's church, but I vividly remember riding to elementary school in my friend's father's dark blue El Camino being told about a book called, *88 Reasons Why the Rapture Will Be in 1988*. I was a ten-year-old boy who had a thirst for end-time knowledge and understanding from the get go, though rest assured that I have researched other beliefs and the validation of an authentic truth comes to fruition in the pages ahead, founded only in the Bible.

With that said, there has not been an instance of time since my childhood that I have ever not believed the rapture would be in my life-time. As I've progressed through life, there have been certain beliefs that keep making their rounds

Introduction

my way. One such misunderstanding about this subject is that it's wasted time to study and teach end-times since people need to know about Jesus, not the rapture. I'm going to shatter that myth!

The two comings of the Lord, the rapture and the Second Coming, are some of the most functional and motivational doctrines in the Bible. The resurrection and the rapture are part of salvation, or one phase of it. If the entire Bible is centered upon salvation and the plan of God for man, then it must be recognized that this subject is not a waste of time and the Holy Spirit inspired many men to tell its story for a reason. They are bona fide motivators to holiness. That is the embodiment of the Great Commission! They teach you to live right daily and to teach others of this event so they will follow the Great Commission and not be caught off guard or be found asleep.

The rapture and Second Coming doctrines are rich with exhortations to be watchful and faithful in hope for the future. They teach death to self so you can have part in the first resurrection, which is the resurrection of the just, finished at least 1,000 years before the end of the second resurrection. The rapture will be to the saints the beginning of eternal and ever increasing splendor, just the beginning of glory that exceeds forevermore in magnificence as time moves forward, but never comes any closer to an end. The Second Coming will take off where the Garden of Eden ceased at the fall of mankind and be the beginning to an endless bliss of fair and just rule, blessing, and favor to Israel and all righteous nations that will be in a state of perpetual perfection for the entire creation from that point on as long as they choose to not rebel against God and His ways.

While looking for my voice to write this book, my mind went in many directions. The final decision came from my heart instead of devising a marketable style. My life from early childhood till now has been filled with the expectation of seeing and being a part of the greatest event of this generation, the rapture. Every fiber of my being for the last 28 years has been that of a watcher's heart.

My voice for the last 12 years has been that of a watcher warning the saints to keep their lanterns full of oil and warning all men to either get right with God or stay right with God, for this is the generation of the rapture, when the plan of God for man advances to the next phase. I'll continue my voice in this five-part series, *Millions Vanished*, with this first book on simply teaching the full doctrine of raptures and resurrections.

You'll learn the differences between a rapture and a resurrection, as well as biblically recorded raptures and resurrections of the past and future. The teaching of the future resurrection of the hybrids of human women and fallen angels is even included for added value. You'll learn everything the Bible has to teach man in this age concerning the catching away of the saints to heaven, as well as all related subjects that must be made known for a full revelation on the subject of raptures and resurrections. The rest of the series will build upon what you learn here. You'll learn truths you had no idea you didn't know.

In the past few years I have believed the prophetic time was sooner than what it really was. The majority don't believe the prophetic time is as late as it really is. I'll teach you how to be prepared no matter how much time is left on God's clock. This present life is short, eternity is forever. Make sure you are preparing for what really matters!

Chapter 1

WHY YOU CAN BELIEVE THE RAPTURE WILL HAPPEN

There's no lack of disbelief and scoffing with the subject of the rapture. The word alone instantly brings an atmosphere of unease, turning expressions to an obvious proclamation of disbelief. People's eyes speak when their mouths remain silent. Isn't all of this for the delusional and religiously insane? After all, the rapture has been talked about for a long time and hasn't happened yet, so it never will, because that belief was for the old timers of intrinsic and charismatic imagination. That's the look I get from almost everyone I speak to in the world, just by mentioning a single word, "rapture."

Now, how do I know the church age will come to an end soon and the Seven Year Tribulation is coming soon? Well, that answer will be thoroughly discussed and proved in book three in the Millions Vanished series. As far as knowing that the rapture will, without any doubt in the universes, come to pass just as surely as the Bible says, I will give you a simple answer. You might be thinking, "Because the Bible tells me so!" That answer is simple, but for many, that is a fictional answer with no validity at all. For the Christian of unwavering faith, it is the only valid answer and nothing more need be said.

My job here is to bridge the gap from unbelief to belief, from seeking to finding, and from mocking to the one being mocked, which turns out to be the best feeling in the world. It feels better to be a fool to the world, instead of a fool to God. To bridge the gap, I won't be focused on proving the Bible to be true, though that will be a result.

First thing to understand is that Jesus had many disciples that followed Him to their own death, many years after His death. Even John was unshakable in faith when Rome boiled him alive, as recorded from secular history. Yet, John suffered no injury, no burns. Jesus also had many others who followed Him to their own death because of their faith that He is the Messiah.

But is the resurrection true? Can the testimonies of those people be believed? The Bible says Jesus was buried, and that he rose again the third day according to the scriptures (1 Cor. 15:4). Some of those scriptures Paul was referring to when writing to the Church of Corinth are as follows: Isaiah 53:13; Ps. 16:10; and Jonah 1:17.

One verse Jesus spoke of is from Jonah, and one of my favorites.

> Now the LORD had prepared a great fish to swallow up Jonah. And Jonah was in the belly of the fish three days and three nights (Jonah 1:17).

> For as Jonas was three days and three nights in the whale's belly; so shall the Son of man be three days and three nights in the heart of the earth (Mat. 12:40).

This verse shows that Jonah was dead for three days and was resurrected as a literal type of Christ. If Jonah was alive in the belly of the whale, then he could not be a true sign of the death and resurrection of Jesus Christ like Jesus was referring to when He said His generation will only receive the sign of the prophet Jonah (Luke 11:29).

But there are those who would ask, "Why should I believe there is a rapture?" The rapture is an event where millions of sinless people on earth will be translated from earth to the sky to meet Jesus. He will then take them bodily to heaven, while changing their bodies to immortality and a state of incorruptibility. Now, I know that statement brings another question. How do people become sinless? I'll be addressing this throughout the book, but specifically in chapters 7 – 8. So all we have so far in explaining why the rapture is a dependable doctrine of truth is that the Bible tells us so.

Let's get back to those witnesses and why their testimony can be believed. There were twelve appearances of Christ after His resurrection: to Mary Magdalene (Mk. 16:9; Jn. 20:15-16), to the women at the tomb (Mat. 28:9), to two disciples on the road to Emmaus (Lk. 24: 13-31), to Peter (Lk. 24:34; 1 Cor. 15:5), to the ten apostles (Jn. 20:19), to the eleven apostles (Jn. 20:26), to the seven apostles (Jn. 21:1-22), to the eleven apostles on a mountain in Galilee (Mat. 28:16), to the twelve apostles, including Matthias (1 Cor. 15:5; Acts 1:26), to five hundred brethren (1 Cor. 15:6), to James, the Lord's brother (1 Cor. 15:7; Gal. 1:19), and to all the apostles (1 Cor. 15:7; Mk. 16:19-20; Lk. 24:50-53; Acts 1:3-12, 26). Simply summarized, over 516 witnesses saw Christ after the resurrection.

An eyewitness account from a credible witness is enough to end a case in court. We have more than 516, and what makes them credible is two-fold. First, these historic accounts were recorded within years and decades of the events surrounding the death, burial, and resurrection of Christ, and in and around the place these events happened. As crazy as these events sound to the unbeliever, and as much as the majority of people in those days wanted to disprove Jesus being the Messiah, they could not. If there was no merit to the astounding claims of a resurrected man who ascended to heaven in front of many, then the story would not have survived past that era. Too many people living in the days of Jesus were still alive when our gospel's were written.

Second, the resurrection of Jesus is the foundation of the Christian faith. If He didn't resurrect, then we serve a dead God like every other religion. Only insane people would follow a man claiming to be God, yet wasn't able to raise Himself from the grave like He claimed He would (Jn. 2:19; Mk. 14:58). The reality is that Christ changed the world. His followers, specifically the twelve disciples, all died a martyr's death except John. Matthias took Judas' place as one of the twelve (Acts 1:26).

According to many 1st and 2nd century historians and theologians, John was placed in boiling oil for entertainment in a coliseum, yet there was not a single burn on his body. It was then that he was sent to the Isle of Patmos, where he was given an unveiling of future events (Rev. 1:1) and wrote the Book of Revelation. Even John was assigned for death in his day for his profession of faith in Jesus Christ. If Jesus was a liar or a lunatic who thought He was the Messiah, but never did come back from the dead, then you would not have such a company of men die for a lie. This means Jesus is Lord.

The apostle Paul was a Christian killer after the reported resurrection until he claims to have seen Jesus with his own eyes. He received many revelations from Jesus in his life and ended up writing 14 of the 27 books found in the New Testament of the Bible. Paul, a former killer of Christians, became a martyr for his belief that Jesus lived a sinless life, died, was buried, and then rose again to be seated at the right hand of God the Father until the rapture of the church and the second phase in the first resurrection (1 Cor. 15:4; 2 Cor. 5:21; Heb. 4:15).

While I haven't even begun to give an extensive defense of the Bible, my quick points will hopefully give the skeptics a reasonable amount of faith in order to believe the rapture will take place just as the Bible claims. If anyone needs an exhausted amount of evidence proving the Bible true from every conceivable angle, then I suggest two books: The Case for Christ by Lee Stroble, and Evidence that Demands a Verdict by Josh McDowell. If Jesus says there's going to be a rapture (Lk. 21:34-36; Jn. 14:1-3; Rev. 3:11), and He in fact did the impossible (Mat. 19:26), then it can be a settled fact in the hearts and minds of everyone that the resurrection of all the dead will happen.

The rapture event can be believed because of the integrity the Bible has already displayed in the realm of prophecy. Some theologians say there are 332 prophecies showing Who the MESSIAH would be/is. Others say there are 456 identifying traits and acts that identify Jesus from prophecy in the Old Testament, written up to 1,700 years before His appointed time to come to earth to fulfill those prophecies. Saving the best for last, I present evidence given from a mathematician as recorded on biblebelievers.org. All but the last paragraph from the rest of this chapter will be from that source.

"After examining only eight different prophecies (Idem, 106), a mathematician and statistician named Stoner conservatively estimated that the chance of one man fulfilling only eight of those prophecies was one in 10^{17}.

To illustrate how large the number 10^{17} is (a figure with 17 zeros), Stoner gave this illustration: If you mark one of ten tickets, and place all the tickets in a hat, and thoroughly stir them, and then ask a blindfolded man to draw one, his chance of getting the right ticket is one in ten. Suppose that we take 10^{17} silver dollars and lay them on the face of Texas. They'll cover all of the state two feet deep. Now mark one of these silver dollars and stir the whole mass thoroughly, all over the state. Blindfold a man and tell him that he can travel as far as he wishes, but he must pick up one silver dollar and say that this is the right one. What chance would he have of getting the right one? Just the same chance that the prophets would've had of writing these eight prophecies and having them all come true in any one man, from their day to the present time, providing they wrote them in their own wisdom (Idem, 106-107).

In financial terms, is there anyone who would not invest in a financial venture if the chance of failure were only one in 10^{17}? This is the kind of sure investment we're offered by god for faith in His Messiah.

From these figures, Professor Stoner, concludes the fulfillment of these eight prophecies alone proves that God inspired the writing of the prophecies (Idem, 107) - the likelihood of mere chance is only one in 10^{17}!

Another way of saying this is that any person who minimizes or ignores the significance of the biblical identifying signs concerning the Messiah would be foolish.

But, of course, there are many more than eight prophecies. In another calculation, Stoner used 48 prophecies (Idem, 109) (even though he could have used Edersheim's 456), and arrived at the extremely conservative estimate that the probability of 48 prophecies being fulfilled in one person is the incredible number 10^{157}. In fact, if anybody can find someone, living or dead, other than Jesus, who can fulfill only half of the predictions concerning the Messiah given in the book "Messiah in Both Testaments" by Fred J. Meldau, the Christian Victory Publishing Company is ready to give a ONE thousand dollar reward! As apologist Josh McDowell says, "There are a lot of men in the universities that could use some extra cash!" (Josh McDowell, Evidence that Demands a Verdict, California: Campus Crusade for Christ, 175).

How large is the number one in 10^{157}? 10^{157} contains 157 zeros! Stoner gives an illustration of this number using electrons. Electrons are very small objects. They're smaller than atoms. It would take 2.5 TIMES 10^{15} of them, laid side by side, to make one inch. Even if we counted 250 of these electrons each minute, and counted day and night, it would still take 19 million years just to count a line of electrons one-inch long (Stoner, op. cit, 109).

With this introduction, let's go back to our chance of one in 10^{157}. Let's suppose that we're taking this number of electrons, marking one, and thoroughly stirring it into the whole mass, then blindfolding a man and letting him try to find the right one. What chance has he of finding the right one? What kind of a pile will this number of electrons make? They make an inconceivably large volume.

This is the result from considering a mere 48 prophecies. Obviously, the probability that 456 prophecies would be fulfilled in one man by chance is vastly smaller. According to Emile Borel, once one goes past one chance in 10^{50}, the probabilities are so small that it is impossible to think that they will ever occur (Ankerberg et. al., op. cit., 21).

As Stoner concludes, 'Any man who rejects Christ as the Son of God is rejecting a fact, proved perhaps more absolutely than any other fact in the world (Stoner, op. cit., 112).'"

More is written here: ***biblebelievers.org.au/radio034.htm***

God so thoroughly vindicated that Jesus is the Christ ('Christ' is Greek for the Hebrew word 'Messiah,' meaning the Anointed One) that even mathematicians and statisticians, who were without faith, had to acknowledge that it is scientifically impossible to deny that Jesus is the Christ. Why can you believe the Rapture, 7 Year Tribulation, the Second Coming, and all the events surrounding them will happen? Because the First Coming happened. The same God that told the prophets to write the 300 – 400 events identifying the first coming of Jesus is the same God that told some of the same men to write of the Second Coming events.

Chapter 2

RAPTURES AND RESURRECTIONS DEFINED AND UNDERSTOOD

Part 1: THE RAPTURE DEFINED AND UNDERSTOOD

The rapture is a word that brings a full barrage of facial expressions when spoken of, from looks of hope and great expectation to looks of dismay and great indignation. There isn't one single broad stroke I can paint to class why there are so many different views and feelings toward one single doctrine. Some hate this historic event that hasn't happened yet because they are afraid. Some love the world more than they love Jesus, therefore want to live their life here first while fulfilling the works of their flesh (Gal. 5:19-21; Jas. 4:4; 1 Jn. 2:15-17). Some want to see their dreams fulfilled, whether the motivation is for more souls in the kingdom or selfish in nature, only God knows.

However, many chase the rapture because they want to be with Jesus more than they love their own life (Mat. 10:37-39; Jn. 14:15-24; 15:10, 14). Many understand the rapture is not going to make anyone forget who they are, forget their life or their friends and family. The rapture will not make anyone look different, other than changing physical imperfections. Many fear those things that are unknown to them. The best way to begin the road to the path of biblical understanding toward the rapture is to first define it and accurately show the rapture in Scripture.

The word "rapture" not being found in the text of the Bible is at the heart of many debates against the doctrine itself. The word rapture simply means to transport from one place to another. The biblical wording equated with rapture is "caught up" (1 Thess. 4:17; 2 Cor. 12:4); "receive you unto myself" (Jn. 14:3); and "come up hither" (Rev. 4:1; 11:12). The word *rapture* is merely a doctrinal term used as a word that has a precise meaning within a particular biblical principle to give a quick reference to a specific belief. I'll make this as simple as I can for you. The word rapture is not in the Bible, but the idea conveyed in Scripture is there. Bible students simply gave it a name.

When the term is used, it simply means the "catching up" of Christians to meet the Lord in the air, who then go to heaven with Jesus to get settled in their eternal mansions (Jn. 14:1-3; Heb. 11:10-16; 13:14; Rev. 3:12). He has gone to prepare a place for those who serve Him until death, or until the time of the rapture (1 Thess. 3:13; 4:13-17; Phil. 3:20-21; Col. 3:4; Jas. 5:7-8). The term "rapture" comes from the Latin verb rapiemur, which means to seize, snatch, or carry away. Many English words have been traced from the Latin language, so this should not concern us. Rapiemur is derived from the Latin root verb rapio, which means to carry off. The English words "rapt" and "rapture" stem from this Latin verb. The New Testament was written mostly in Greek at the time of its origin.

There are more than one Greek equivalents to the word rapture, meaning many Greek words are used in describing the event of the rapture, just like many English words have been used to do the same. We have already given some English words above, like "caught up," "receive you unto myself," and "come up hither." The Greek word most commonly associated with the rapture is harpazo, which has the same meaning as the Latin word rapiemur, to seize, snatch, or carry away. The most famous passage on the rapture uses the word harpazo when written in the original Greek.

> For the Lord himself shall descend from heaven with a shout, with the voice of the archangel, and with the trump of God: and the dead in Christ shall rise first: Then we which are alive and remain shall be <u>caught up</u> (harpazo) together with them in the clouds, to meet the Lord in the air: and so shall we ever be with the Lord (1 Thess. 4:16-17).

From the word "harpazo" the term "rapture" is derived, meaning the act of transporting. The word harpazo is used elsewhere in scripture and has nothing to do with the rapture event as we think of it. Just to fully understand the use of this word we'll look at a couple verses, although there are over a dozen verses.

> When any one heareth the word of the kingdom, and understandeth it not, then cometh the wicked one, and <u>catcheth away</u> (harpazo) that which was sown in his heart. This is he which received seed by the way side (Mt. 13:19).

This is a direct reference to those who have received the truth of the Word of God, but did not fully understand it, allowing Satan to easily take that truth away, or pluck it away from them.

Do you see what this word harpazo means? When used in other context, it simply means the same thing as in the rapture context. Let's not overlook the plain truth of Matthew 13:19 as we do a word study, since the context is relevant to our topic. These truths I'm presenting are to be understood or else they would not be spoken of as much as they are in the Bible. I've seen this throughout my life with the end-time subjects. When a good understanding is not clear and present, the enemy comes and <u>catches it away</u> (harpazo).

Try one more from John 10. "And I give unto them eternal life; and they shall never perish, neither shall any man <u>pluck</u> (harpazo) them out of my hand." [pluck] Greek: *harpazo* (GSN-<G726>), take by force (Mat. 11:12; Jn. 6:15; Acts 23:10); catch (Jn. 10:12); catch away or up (Mat. 13:19; Acts 8:39; 2 Cor. 12:2-4; 1 Thess. 4:17; Rev. 12:5); pull (Jude 1:23); and pluck (Jn. 10:28-29).

The intention of the preceding study of the Latin, Greek, and English words for the doctrine of the rapture is to emphasis that language should not be a reason to dismiss any concept that is established in Scripture just because the doctrinal term is not in the Bible. What is important is that the concept is found since other terms synonymous with rapture are found in the Bible. If we were to have this misunderstanding with all doctrinal terms or regular words in general, then there would be nothing but fruitless debating while the truths we are supposed to learn would all be hid or taken away by the wicked one (Mat.13:19).

For example, the essential doctrine of the trinity would be distorted and / or unlearned if we doubted the body of teachings advocated by hundreds of clear verses proclaiming the truth of three separate Beings in unity that all hold the title, God (Gen. 1:26; 3:22; 11:7; 19:24; Ex. 14:19; 23:20-23; 32:34; 33:1-3; Num. 20:16; Deut. 18:15-19; Ps.. 2:1-12; 8:3-6; 16:8-11; 22:1-31; 34:20; 45:6-7; 68:18; 69:8-9; 89:27; 110:1-5; 118:26; 119:97-104; 132:11, 17; Prov. 30:4; Isa. 7:14; 8:18; 9:6-7; 11:1-5; 42:1-7; 49:1-12; 50:4-11; 52:13-15; 53:1-

12; 55:4-5; 63:1-10; Jer. 23:5-8; Ezek. 33:15-18; 34:29; Dan. 7:9-14; Hos. 11:1; Mic. 5:1-6; Hab. 2:7; Zech. 6:12-13; 12:10; 13:6, 7; Mal. 3:1-3; Mat. 1:20-25; 3:9-17; 4:1-11; 12:18-21; 6 16-17; 22:42-46; 28:19-20; Mark 1:10-11; 12:35-37; Luke 1:32-35, 67-80; 2:25-35, 38; 3:22; 11:9-13; 24:49; John 1:31-34; 3:34-36; 14:16-21, 23-26; 15:26; 16:7-17; 20:21-23; Acts 1:1-8; 2:17-21, 33-39; 4:8-12, 24-31; 5:30-32; 6:1-15; 7:1-53; 7:54-56; 8:5-23, 29-39; 9:5-20; 10:2-48; 11:15-25; 13:2-12, 46-52; 15:7-29; 18:24-28; 20:21-35; Rom. 4:1-4; 5:1-5; 8:1-27; 9:1-5; 14:17-18; 15:8-30; 1 Cor. 2:1-15; 3:16-23; 6:9-19; 7:22-24, 40; 12:1-29; 2 Cor. 1:18-23; 3:3-18; 5: 1-10; 6:1-18; 13:14; Gal. 3:1-11; 4:7; 5:16-26; 6:2-8; Eph. 1:3-21; 4:3-32; 5:1-21, 6:6-24; Phil. 1:1-19; 2:1-11; Col. 1:3-8; 1 Thess. 1:1-10; 4:1-18; 5:9-28; 2 Thess. 2:13-17; 1 Tim. 3:15-17; 4:1-10; 2 Tim. 1:6-14; Titus 3:4-7; Heb. 2:1-14; 3:1-12; 6:1-6; 9:6-14; 10:10-18, 26-31; 1 Pt. 1:1-4, 10-25; 3:15-22; 4:13-19; 2 Pet. 1:16-21; 1 John 3:23-24; 4:2-3, 12-16; 5:5-11; Jude 20-21; Rev. 1:4-6, 9-10; 3:1-13, 21-22; 4:1-3; 5:1-10; 11:3-13; 14:12-13; 19:1-10; 22:16-21; etc.).

Also not found in the King James Bible are the words Bible, demon, omnipresent, omniscience, animal, and a lot more. Can you imagine not believing in animals because the word is not in the Bible? The truth of animals in Scripture is undoubtedly seen. The belief of the Second Coming is believed by most professing Christians, yet that term cannot be found anywhere in the Bible. Also, the term "Millennial Reign" is not in the Bible, yet it is a true future event easily seen in Scripture (Rev. 20:2-7).

The original text in which the language was written reveals the authenticity and validity to the rapture doctrine. No one needs to devise a lie, as some believe, that it was invented in 1830 by a man named John Darby. Can man make up a doctrine today that can't be validated by the original text and expect people to believe it? No, but just as sure as I write this, someone is believing a doctrine that cannot be harmonized in the original text of the Bible.

I have a more sure faith in the readers of this series. I believe you picked up this book on purpose and by the power of the Holy Spirit. The time is close and all who call themselves a child of God need to strengthen themselves in knowledge, truth and understanding of the times ahead. If you gain nothing else from this chapter, just remember that the rapture of the church is merely the "catching up" of the righteous to meet Jesus in the air to go to heaven for a time of at least seven years.

While introducing the rapture doctrine to some of you, many are very familiar with the term already. A few reading this will already believe what they've heard about the rapture doctrine from some famous teachers who hold that the church will be raptured after the Tribulation (using Mt. 24:29-31). The ecumenical belief of the church in all ages is that the church will go from tribulation to glory. They simply hand down a false understanding that the pre-tribulation rapture teaching was popularized in 1830 by a man named John Darby. These teachers believe the rapture did not exist before it "popped into John Darby's head" and no one had ever heard of a secret rapture doctrine before this. The truth is that Darby did not invent this doctrine that can be clearly seen in the New Testament. We will be emphatically proving this throughout these pages.

John Darby may have discovered it for himself, or with a Bible teacher showing him these truths, but he did not make it up. I really do not know where or when Darby learned this doctrine. Without learning a thing from Darby's writings, I learned these truths from the Scripture by examining what I had been taught by man. This is what we must all do (Acts 17:11; 2 Tim. 2:15). In fact, the pre-tribulation rapture was first mentioned by Jesus, and then was taught by Luke, John, Paul, Peter, and James in their writings found in the New Testament that had been consummated more than 1,700 years before 1830 and the day of John Darby.

The rapture finds its origins in the pages of the Holy Spirit inspired text of the Bible and proclaims the catching away of the Old Testament saints and the church saints. This will be fulfilled at least seven years prior to the Second Coming of Christ. All those absolute statements will be presented in detail and clearly proven in the next chapters, but to say that this doctrine was first discovered in 1830 is like saying that justification by faith is an invention from a man named Martin Luther in 1517. The fact is both these doctrines have been taught from the scriptures and neither were invented in 1517 or 1830.

What would happen if we take that mentality with us when coming across every situation? Naturally, that is nonsense that would leave us ignorant and unreasonable with even the most logical of reasoning. The analytically minded would want to beat their head against a wall when talking to anyone when diving below surface level information of any kind. Shall we also believe Christopher Columbus was really the first man who discovered North America while we purposefully become willfully ignorant about the Native Americans already living here? Let us just remain as reasonable as God created us to be.

Let's go back to the word "rapture" not being found in the Bible. Many people say it is not a biblical doctrine due to that fact, but we have proven thus far that it is. Because of the word rapture not being in the Bible, many doubters of the rapture event also doubt man is going to heaven before the Second Coming. Many scriptures speak plainly of people being in heaven in between the rapture and the Second Coming. John 14:1-3 lets us know that Jesus is going to prepare a place for the righteous in His Father's house, which is one of the names of the holy city, New Jerusalem. Jesus says He will come get the righteous and take them where He is, which is in heaven, where He is (1 Pet. 3:22; Rev. 1:1; 19:1-16).

Revelation 5:8-10 lets us know that there will be 24 crowned elders in heaven after the rapture (Rev. 4:1-4), but before the 7 Year Tribulation (Rev. 6 – Rev. 22). These 24 elders are representatives for all saints at this that, proven by the fact that they are redeemed to God by thy blood out of every kindred, and tongue, and people, and nation and God has made them kings and priests who will reign on the earth. Now, those elders have crowns (Rev. 4:4), and the saints are made kings and priests, so it must be understood that the rapture had already happened since the judgment seat of Christ will be after the saints are glorified at the time of the rapture (Lk. 14:14; 1 Cor. 3:12-15; 9:24-27; 2 Cor. 5:10-11; Col. 3:24). Revelation 14:1-5 and many other scriptures also clearly show people in heaven before the Second Coming (Rev. 19:11-16). Two men are even in heaven right now in their mortal bodies (Gen. 5:24; Zech. 4:14; 2 Kings 2; Mal. 4:5-6; Rev. 11:3-12).

One quick note to point out about people going to heaven after the rapture and even after the Second Coming is that the glorified saints will be reigning and ruling the earth with Jesus during the thousand years after the Second Coming and forever more (Dan. 7:13-14, 18, 27). However, the home Jesus spoke of for all reigning saints is in the Holy City, also called "My Father's House" (Jn. 14:1-3). The Holy City, the New Jerusalem, will be transferred to earth after the thousand years (Rev. 21 – Rev. 22), but until then, the saints will be going to and fro from heaven to earth, from earth to heaven. Speculation says the saints will travel at the speed of thought, but no solid scripture can be presented. One thing for sure is that the glorified saint will have access to heaven indefinitely.

I had previously mentioned that Jesus was the first one to mention the rapture (Jn. 14:1-3; Lk. 21:34-36), though He was not the one who directly taught the doctrine. Paul was the first to reveal this mystery as seen in 1 Thessalonians 2:19; 3:13; 4:13-18; 5:9, 23; 1 Cor. 15:23; 51-54, and in other books of the Bible. I say this to bring up one of the many fallacies taught in the past few decades, which is that Jesus never once mentioned the rapture, much less a separate and distinct coming aside from the Second Coming. As taught already, John pens the words of Jesus Himself in John 14:1-3 and lets his disciples know that He would come and take all the saints to heaven to live with Him before He sets up His kingdom on earth.

In another instance, Jesus even told His disciples that all His faithful followers will escape all the things happening on the earth during the end-time events of the 7 Year Tribulation at the end of this age and stand before Him (Lk. 21:34-36). Some people mock the pre-tribulation rapture by calling it escapism. Luke 21:36 clearly teaches an escape for the worthy ones. A few decades after Jesus' earthly ministry, He also told John that the church would be caught up to heaven before the wrath of God is poured out on the earth (Rev. 1:19; 4:1). The pre-tribulation rapture is addressed throughout this book, but pin-pointed further in book two, *7 Rapture Views*.

Part 2: THE RESURRECTION DEFINED AND UNDERSTOOD

I'm still ceased to be amazed by the assertions concerning what is and is not found in the Bible. There really is nothing new under the sun. People were saying the same thing in Corinth during the early church and Paul's life. There really are those who claim the teaching of a resurrection is not scriptural, or that it has already happened (2 Thess. 2:1-12).

> Now if Christ be preached that he rose from the dead, <u>how say some among you that there is no resurrection of the dead</u>? But if there be no resurrection of the dead, then is Christ not risen: And if Christ be not risen, then *is* our preaching vain, and your faith *is* also vain (1 Cor. 15:12-14).

Many Bible people confirm their belief in the resurrection. Some are of the faith and some are not: Job (19:25-27), Isaiah (16:14-19), Daniel (12:3), David (Ps. 16:17:15; Acts 2:31), Old Testament Saints (Heb. 11:35), New Testament Saints (Mat. 28; Mk. 16; Lk. 24; Jn. 20-21; Acts 2; 4; etc.), Jesus (Mat. 16:21; 22:23-31; Lk. 14:14; 20:27-36; 24:13-35), Matthew (28:1-20), Mark (16:1-18), Luke (24:1-49) John (19-21; Rev. 20:4-6), Mary (John 11:24), Herod (Mat. 14:2), Peter (1 Pt. 1:3; 3:21), Paul (Acts 17:18, 32; 23:6; 24:15, 21; Rom. 1:4; 6:5; 8:34; 1 Cor. 15; Phil. 3:10-11; Heb. 6:2; 11:35).

When many people think of a resurrection, they think of people who have physically died coming back to life by the power of God. This familiar definition is the simplest and most straight forward. With this, I want to make the distinction between the rapture and the resurrection before we move on, or more accurately stated as *a* rapture or *a* resurrection.

Raptures and Resurrections Defined and Understood

Many people believe the resurrection is synonymous with the rapture, and if they are referring to the rapture of the dead in Christ who precede the saints who are physically alive on earth at the time of the trumpet sound, then they are correct (1 Thess. 3:13; 4:13-14). What they don't know is there have been and will be more resurrections and raptures than the famous and widely anticipated rapture of the church.

Not all raptures have included, or will include a resurrection; however, all eternal raptures for the righteous will include, or have already included, a changing of the natural body to the glorified condition. Also, not all raptures have resulted in a change of the body to its eternal state. Basically, there are natural and eternal raptures and resurrections. Some take place at the same moment, while others occur independently from each other. Sometimes one will occur without the other.

This may be making your eyebrows squint in confusion, but this will be easily picked up and understood by reading along with the outlines in chapter 4. For the Bible believer, what you are about to learn will be exactly what you've always wanted in a rapture teaching. For the seekers looking for answers about the afterlife, or if God has a plan for the future of mankind, this is the hope and truth you've been looking for. Look over these basic outlines in chapter 4 and refer back to them to make following along painless.

Chapter 3

REASONS FOR THE RAPTURE OF THE CHURCH AND THE TRIBULATION

Purposes for the rapture are given throughout Scripture. They are numerous and wonderful for all who choose to follow Jesus, but offer no hope for those who reject Him and His ways. For many profess to believe in God, know Him, and be one of His children, but few are known by Him.

> Whosoever transgresseth, and abideth not in the doctrine of Christ, hath not God. He that abideth in the doctrine of Christ, he hath both the Father and the Son (2 Jn. 9).

> And hereby we do know that we know him, if we keep his commandments. He that saith, I know him, and keepeth not his commandments, is a liar, and the truth is not in him (1 Jn. 2:3-4).

Few will step on the narrow path, and even fewer still remain on that path to walk through the narrow gate at death or rapture (Mat. 7:13-14; 1 Pt. 4:17-19). This is because of sin and iniquity found in a believer's life when they go against the will of God (Mat. 7:21-23; 1 Jn. 1:5-7; 3:1-10; 5:1-18). We will learn why the rapture must happen, but in the midst of it all, we will learn what it means to be a believer of Christ, and a follower of Christ. Many profess to be a part of the kingdom, but few possess the kingdom of heaven. Be a follower, not a believer only (Jas. 1:22-25). By the end of this book, you'll be completely equipped to be an overcomer and possessor of the kingdom.

The main purpose for the rapture of the church cannot be fully understood unless we can understand the purpose for the Seven Year Tribulation. For starters, the main purpose for the rapture is to bring an end to the church age so the Tribulation, or Daniel's 70th Week, can begin. Jesus Christ will receive the saints of all past ages to Himself (Jn. 14:1-3). The 70th week is the last seven years of this dispensation (Dan. 9:27; Rev. 6:1 – Rev. 19:10), beginning after the rapture (Rev. 4:1) and ending before the Second Coming (Rev. 19:11-21).

The rapture is the ending of this age, called the Church Age. A dispensation is a specific period of time, while an age is any period of time, whether long or short. This is how the Dispensation of Grace continues a few years after the Church Age ends. The Dispensation of Divine Government, also called the Millennial Reign, is the next dispensation, which lasts for one thousand years (Rev. 20:1-15). The final dispensation will be after the Millennial Reign in the New Heavens and the New Earth.

It could be called, the Dispensation of the Redeemed Humans and Faithful Angels. At that time God's original purpose will be fully accomplished when man lives as intended before the fall (Gen. 1:26-28). His purpose for man was not destroyed by the fall (Gen. 2:17, 25; 3:1-19), just delayed (Rev. 21 – Rev. 22). This is not to say God didn't know this would happen, for He laid out the plan of redemption before the foundation of the world (Mat. 13:35; Rom. 8:29-30; Eph. 1:4-5; 1 Pt. 1:20).

There will finally be a universe void from any possibility of rebellion, like with Lucifer's uprising and sinful existence (Isa. 14:12-14; Ezek. 28:11-17; Mat. 25:41; Jn. 8:44; 10:10;

1 Jn. 3:8-10), and like all humans have done by every act of sin (Ex. 32:33; Rom. 3:23; Jas. 4:4; 1 Jn. 2:15-17). The eternal future will be free from sin, rebellion, and all fear of death, for there will be no death, and every tear will be wiped away. The Dispensation of the Redeemed Humans and Faithful Angels will be an eternal government exclusively ruled by God the Father, God the Son, God the Holy Spirit, and the redeemed human beings and the faithful angels (Rev. 21:1 – Rev. 22:5; 1 Cor. 15:24-28).

The Seven Year Tribulation, or Daniel's 70th Week (Dan.9:27), will see the fulfillment of all of Matthew 24 – Matthew 25; Revelation 4 – Revelation 19; Daniel 7:19-27; 8:9-14, 22-25; 9:27; 11:36-45; and many other passages. The last half of the Tribulation is called The Great Tribulation, or Jacob's Trouble, and will be during the last half of the Seven Year Tribulation, lasting three and a half years (Dan. 9:27; 11:40-45; 12:1, 7, 11; Jer. 30:4-7; Rev. 7:14; 11:1 – Rev. 19:21). The first half of the Tribulation will be extremely bad, but will be a lesser tribulation due to the fact that Antichrist will only be rising to power (Daniel 7:23-24; Matthew 24:4-14; Rev. 6:1 – Rev. 9:21). The focus of Daniel's Seventieth Week is on Israel, so when the Antichrist breaks treaty with Israel and seeks to annihilate them, it will be a greater tribulation for them (Mat. 24:15-21).

To fully understand the seven years of tribulation, we have to understand the prophecy of Daniel's seventy weeks.

> 24 <u>Seventy weeks</u> are determined upon <u>thy people and upon thy holy city</u>, to finish the transgression, and to make an end of sins, and to make reconciliation for iniquity, and to bring in everlasting righteousness, and to seal up the vision and prophecy, and to anoint the most Holy. 25 Know therefore and understand, *that* from the going forth of the

commandment to restore and to build Jerusalem unto the Messiah the Prince *shall be* <u>seven weeks</u>, and <u>threescore and two weeks</u>: the street shall be built again, and the wall, even in troublous times. 26 <u>And after</u> threescore and two weeks shall Messiah be cut off, but not for himself: and the people of the prince that shall come shall destroy the city and the sanctuary; and the end thereof *shall be* with a flood, and unto the end of the war desolations are determined. 27 <u>And he shall confirm the covenant with many for one week</u>: and <u>in the midst of the week</u> he shall cause the sacrifice and the oblation to cease, and for the overspreading of abominations he shall make *it* desolate, even until the consummation, and that determined shall be poured upon the desolate (Dan. 9:24-27).

    I have friends and family members that don't understand, or even know about, Daniel's seventy weeks, even though they've been in church their whole lives. I can't say how amazed I am by that reality, and I'll tell you why. Over three hundred prophecies were written in the Old Testament that all identify the One who is our life and our salvation (Jn. 14:6; 1 Jn. 5:20). As said before, these prophecies began being foretold in the garden immediately after the fall of the human race (Gen. 3:15).

    One such passage undeniably identifies the author and finisher of our faith by precisely telling us when He would be crucified. The seventy weeks prophecy of Daniel is one of the most irrefutable text proofs of the claims of Jesus being the messiah, so much so that those practicing Judaism argue over the proper translation of Daniel 9:24-27 in the King James Version. They go so far as to change the history of when the command to restore Jerusalem really happened (Dan. 9:25).

    If all agreed with historical time lines, then all would believe that Jesus is the Messiah (Anointed One). Have you ever wondered how the magi, "the three wise men," knew it was time for the Messiah? Yes, there was a star that led them, but they were expecting Him before the star appeared. These magi were followers of God and had His holy Word. They understood prophecy, obviously believing in the coming King, and understood recent history, as it was from their perspective as you'll soon learn. Understanding history and learning this amazing prophecy would let you know exactly when Jesus would be killed, but not born.

First, when do the seventy weeks begin? With the commandment "to restore and to build Jerusalem unto the Messiah the Prince" (Dan. 9:25). History reveals three decrees for the restoration of Jerusalem. By understanding the specific one referred to in Daniel 9, we can know the exact year of the crucifixion, for being cut off is always a reference to death, (Dan. 9:26). It must be clear that Jesus' age was never foretold in Scripture, therefore the wise men didn't know when He would be born.

Follow me for a minute and you'll not only have the proper understanding of the seventy weeks and how dynamic they are in understanding the Seven Year Tribulation, but also understand why this is one of the greatest Messianic prophecies in Scripture that all in the faith should learn. The first decree was given during the first year of the reign of Cyrus, king of Persia (Ezra 1:1-4; 3:8; Isa. 44:28; 45:1-4; 46:11), which is who some Jews believe to be "Messiah the Prince" in Daniel 9:25. Cyrus reigned 9 years; then Cambyses, his son, reigned 7 years. In the son's reign the work on the temple ceased (Ezra 4:1-24).

According to secular history, Darius I reigned 35 years. In the second year of his reign he confirmed the decree Cyrus had made 18 years before. The temple was finished in the sixth year of his reign, but the city was not restored. Xerxes reigned 21 years (Dan. 11:1-3), during which time the city was not yet completed. Artaxerxes reigned for 40 years. In the 20th year of his reign (444 B.C.) he gave Nehemiah the 3rd decree "to restore and to build Jerusalem unto the Messiah the Prince" (Dan. 9:25-26; Neh. 2:1 – Neh. 6:19). This is the point in time when the 70 weeks, or 490 years are counted.

The seventy weeks are divided into three divisions. Daniel 9:25 gives the first section, which lasts for seven weeks, or literally forty-nine years. We understand the length of the seventy weeks as 70 periods of 7 years. The phrase "seventy weeks" literally means "seventy sevens." Hebrew for "week" is SHABUWA (HEBREW STRONG'S NUMBER: 7620), seven. We know the "weeks," or periods of sevens, is referring to years, not days, because Daniel's prayer, to which this vision was an answer, concerned years, not days (Dan. 9:2). This is how we get forty-nine years from seven weeks. Seven weeks is seven periods of seven years, or seven times seven.

So, seventy weeks is a period of time lasting 490 years, because 70 times seven years equals 490 years. Daniel 9:25 began to be fulfilled when Nehemiah restored the walls in 52 days after he got to Jerusalem. That took place during the next 49 years. In short, the third decree to restore Jerusalem was 92 years after the decree given by Cyrus, which was the first decree according to (Ezra 1:1-4; 3:8; Isa. 44:28; 45:1-4; 46:11).

With the first division of 7 weeks accomplished, the second division of the seventy weeks is a period of 62 weeks, or 434 years from the completion of Jerusalem at the end of the forty-nine years to the time the Messiah is cut off, or killed, which we know to be by crucifixion (Dan. 9:25-26; Isa. 53). The total amount of weeks (periods of seven years) from the beginning of the restoring of Jerusalem until when the Messiah the Prince (Jesus) was to be cut off (killed), is 69 weeks, or 483 years.

By knowing that simple prophecy combined with the history that was extremely significant in their day, only being about 450 years old at it's furthest point, it would easily tell the wise men that the Messiah was to be born soon. You see, Jesus was to be born 450 years after the decree to restore and build Jerusalem, because He was to be cut off 483 years after that decree and He was 33 when He was crucified. The "three" wise men didn't know He would be 33 since this was never revealed in Scripture, but they knew the Messiah would be a man, so they must have been expecting Him to be born for years. There is no difference in application with watching for His coming in the air to receive His saints. What if the magi, "three wise men," grew weary of waiting and watching?

The third division of the prophecy of Daniel's Seventy Weeks is one week, or seven years, which is the last seven years of this age. The beginning of this week, or Seven Year Tribulation (Rev. 6:1 – Rev. 19:10), begins with the revealing of the Antichrist (Dan. 9:27; 2 Thess. 2:3-4, 7-8; Rev. 6:2) after the rapture of the church (Rev. 4:1), and ends with the Second Coming of Christ (Rev. 19:11-21) to fulfill the six events of Daniel 9:24.

Daniel's 70th Week was given for the people of Israel, so there must not be debate over the gap of time interrupting the 69 weeks and the 70th. Israel rejected their Messiah and was cut off (Rom. 11:17-24). The church was never hinted at in the entire Old Testament and only came into existence during Jesus' earthly ministry. The church is what is happening in between these last two periods of Daniel's 70 Weeks. Once the church is raptured, God brings His whole focus back toward

Israel in order to bring them to repentance and aligned under the terms of the new covenant.

Since we know the last half of the Tribulation is 3.5 years (Rev. 11:1-3; 12:6, 14; 13:5; Dan. 7:25; 12:7), then we can clearly see the whole of the Tribulation is double that, or 7 years (Dan. 9:27). If the last division of the seventy weeks is a period of 7 years, then the other "weeks" are also 7 years each. Therefore, we can conclusively say the whole period is 490 years (70 x 7 = 490 years). This is how the term "Seven Year Tribulation" came about, and believing in the Tribulation and not understanding its origin founded in Daniel 9 is why I am concerned for the church.

We aren't sure why we believe what we learn, or even how to locate our beliefs in Scripture. This is how so many who profess Christ are deceived with different Christs, and different gospels that leave people damned (Mat. 24:4-5; Gal. 1:6-9; 2 Cor. 11:3-4, 12-15). Followers of Christ are repeatedly given many warnings against being deceived (Mat. 24:4-5, 11, 24; Lk. 21:8; 1 Cor. 6:9; 15:33; Gal. 6:7; Eph. 5:6; 2 Thess. 2:3). We have to be able to back up what we believe, because it might just be a deception.

The purpose of the rapture is to resurrect the just from the dead and take all the saints out of the world before Daniel's last week comes. The rapture seems like a fairy tale to the world, and I'm talking about friends in the world I've made over the years that literally believe in the zombie apocalypse. The rapture must happen in order to consummate the plan of God.

The simple truth is God has put mankind on a probationary period in order to know who will choose Him or not, by their own free will. There must be an appointed time for everything, and there is. Even the physical body of God dwelling on earth with man for eternity has an appointed time line that God knows and is the one who ordained it in His plan of salvation (Rev. 21 – Rev. 22).

The rapture will happen in order that His saints may fulfill in them the purpose for which God has saved them. Jesus told the disciples that some would escape the terrible things that were to transpire on the earth in the last days. He said, "Pray that ye may be accounted worthy to escape all these things (things from Matthew 24 – Matthew 25; Luke 21:1-19, 25-28) that shall come to pass, and to stand before the Son of man" (Lk. 21:34-36). This passage is much the same in heart and soul as John 14:1-3.

God will give His faithful servants the inheritance of eternal life as His adopted sons and daughters, not only children, but also heirs (Rom. 8:17; Eph. 3:6; Heb. 11:9; 1 Pet. 3:7). This probationary period is even going to continue on into the Millennial Reign to test the people born in those years. The final exam is at the end of the thousand years when God releases Satan and all his companions in order to tempt the natural people of that day to see if they will rebel against Jesus and His glorified people. Many will have it in their heart to sin and deny the righteous standard that is actually enforced by law throughout the whole earth.

It is the love of God that spills out of His plan for man. The plan has different phases, or dispensations that all play on one another, each one in its own order. There must be a resurrection of all the dead in Christ for the completion of His plan to come. Jesus and His ruling saints must all be glorified and immortal to take back the earth and rule it in righteousness forever. But what about the living in Christ at the time of the rapture? Well, to be fair and impartial, God will at that time bring the living in Christ up in the sky to meet Him and be as He is (1 Thess. 4:16-17; 1 Jn. 3:1-3).

Now, what about the man child, or the 144,000 of Revelation 12:5? What about the great multitude of tribulation saints in heaven? Will they come to earth in spirit form on white horses to rule and reign with the glorified church saints? What about the two witnesses who are resurrected and raptured to heaven in front of many eyes? Will they be a part of the first resurrection (Rev. 20:4-6) and rule with Christ? Of course, for all in Christ will be resurrected and/or raptured in his own order (1 Cor. 15:20, 23). God has a plan, and it is so good that the sci-fi enthusiast can't even fathom it.

God has a purpose. The purpose of the Tribulation is to purify Israel and bring the nation back to a place where God can fulfill the everlasting covenants made with the fathers of Israel (Isa. 2:6; 3:26; 16:1-5; 24:1-23; 26:20-21; Ezek. 20:33-34; 22:17-22; Rom. 11:25-29). Like God's plan for man before the fall, rebellion of Israel did not annihilate the covenant, it just postponed it. But let's not be confused about salvation in any aspect. Not all of Israel will be saved in times past regarding individual Jews.

It is appointed once for man to die, then the judgment (Heb. 9:27). How you die is how you remain for eternity (Rev. 22:11). All of Israel at the time of the Second Coming will be saved physically and spiritually (Rom. 11:25-29), because they will be fighting the largest and most powerful assembled military force in history on that day. It would surely destroy them, but Jesus and His mighty angel army and all glorified saints will be seen in the sky to defend Israel, and then Israel will say, "Hosanna, blessed is He who comes in the name of the Lord (Ps. 118:26, partially fulfilled at Jesus' first coming and quoted in Mt. 21:9; 23:39; Mk. 11:9; Lk. 13:35; 19:38; Jn. 12:13).

Part of the purpose for the Tribulation will be to purify Israel of all enemies (Ezek. 20:33-34; 22:17-22; Zech. 13:8-9; Mal. 3:3-4; Mat. 25:31-46) and bring them into the bond of the new covenant (Ezek. 20:33-34; 36:24-28; Jer. 30:3-11; Zech. 12:10 – Zech. 13:9; Mal. 4:3-4). People of all faiths, even many Christians, have denied Bible truth that Israel has a unique place in God's heart. I mean, just look at how ungodly they are. How can they have God the Father while rejecting God the Son? Well, that's easy. They cannot (Ezek. 18:24-26; Isa. 59:1-2; Jn. 3:36; 14:6; Rom. 11:17-25; 2 Jn. 1:9).

Other prominent men have gone the other extreme and actually written in books that evangelizing Israel is the biggest waste of time a Christian can do when following the Great Commission, because Jesus never came to be the Messiah to the Jewish people. Israel has their own covenant that secures them. Both trains of thought are easily derailed with Scripture throughout the Bible. There is no salvation in any other than Jesus (Jn. 14:6; Acts 4:12; 1 Jn. 5:20), and the old covenant was abolished, done away with, and annulled on the cross (Rom. 10:4; 2 Cor. 3:6-15; Gal. 3:13-25; 4:21-31; Eph. 2:15; Col. 2:14-17; Heb. 8:7-13; 10:9). The new covenant was made for all men and women by the blood of Jesus (Mat. 26:28; Mk. 14:24; Jn. 3:16; Acts 20:28; Rom. 3:24-25; Eph. 1:7; 2:13-16; Rev. 1:5-6; 5:9; 12:11; 22:17).

Israelis, Hebrews, Jews, or whatever you believe to be the correct word to categorize the descendants of Abraham, Isaac, and Jacob, will all be individually judged according to their standing with God through Jesus Christ alone (Eph. 2:1-10). Daniel's 70th Week will permit the coming of the man of sin (2 Thess. 2:7-8), which will cause Israel to flee into the wilderness of Edom and Moab (modern-day Jordan) when the Antichrist breaks his seven-year covenant with them and seeks to destroy them all. This will actually bring Israel back to God, for they will turn to Him for help (Isa. 16:1-5; Ezek. 20:33-35; Dan. 11:40 – Dan.12:7; Hos. 2:14-17; Mat. 24:15-31; Rev. 12).

Again, make no critical error in the doctrine of salvation, for the Tribulation is also equally a time to judge Israel for their rejection of the Messiah and make them willing to accept Him when He comes the second time to the earth (Ezek. 20:22, 34; Zech. 12:10 – Zech. 13:9; 14:1-15; Mat. 24:15-31). At that time, Jesus will judge the nations for their persecution of Israel (Isa. 16:3-5; Joel 3; Rev. 6:1 – Rev. 19:21) after Israel was brought back to God by complete repentance (Ezek. 18:24-32; Zech. 12:10 – Zech. 13:9; Rom. 11:26-29; Mat. 23:39).

A heavy purpose for the rapture is to take saints off of the earth for the duration of the Tribulation (Lk. 21:34-36) in order to end the church age and make it manageable for God to deal more exclusively with Israel to fulfill with them the last day prophecies (Dan. 9:27; 11:4-45; Zech. 12:1 – Zech. 14:15; Mat. 24 – Mat. 25; Lk. 21:1-11, 25-33; 2 Thess. 2; Rev. 1:19; 4:1). This purpose will free saints from the coming wrath of God (1 Thess. 5:1-11) when Jesus receives the fruit of the early and latter rain (Jas. 5:7-8). That is to say the saints who have died from all ages past until the very last one before the resurrection of all Old and New Testament saints, whether Israel, the church, or gentile.

All saints will be given final salvation and grace (Rom. 13:11; 1 Pet. 1:5, 7, 9, 13), which will reveal the glory of God and Christ to them (1 Pt. 4:13), while also giving the saints a reckoning day (1 Pt. 4:5-6). All are purposed for an appointed time in the soon future. For the plan of God for man to advance, the rapture must take place for the saints to be presented to God in heaven (1 Thess. 3:13), whole in body, soul, and spirit (1 Thess. 5:23) to settle the saints into their mansions (Jn. 14:1-3; Heb. 11:10-16; 12:22-23; Heb. 13:14), and confirm them blameless (1 Cor. 1:8; 1 Thess. 3:13; 5:23) before Him for eternity (Rev. 22:11). People are designed to be whole in body, soul, and spirit, not to merely live in heaven in spirit-soul form.

The saints will receive victory over death, hell, and the grave (1 Cor. 15:51-56) when all in Christ at that moment will be given unforfeitable, everlasting life (Gal. 6:7-8), which completes the work started in saints (Phil. 1:6). All resurrected saints of the New Testament and Old Testament (1 Cor. 15:23, 35-44; 2 Cor. 4:14; Phil. 3:11; Dan. 12:2; Jn. 5:28-29; 1 Thess. 4:13-18; Rev. 20:4-6) will rise from their vile body to be like Christ (Phil. 3:21; 1 Jn. 3:2) in order to be judged at the judgment seat of Christ (Rom. 14:10-12; 1 Cor. 3:11-15; 2 Cor. 5:10; Phil. 3:10-11; 2 Tim. 4:1, 8) and assigned positions as kings and priests to rule all creation (1 Cor. 6:1-3; Lk. 22:30; Rev. 1:5; 2:26-27; 5:10; Ps. 8; Dan. 7:1-27).

God will present the church to Himself (Eph. 5:27), making the blessed hope realized by complete fulfillment (Tit. 2:11-13). There will be great joy to soul winners (1 Thess. 2:19-20; 2 Cor. 1:14), and a heavier head after receiving a crown of righteousness (2 Tim. 4:8). Different glories will be received for the many saints (1 Cor. 15:23, 35-44), but our body will be able to stand tall with the weight of reward, for we will be changed from mortality to immortality (1 Cor. 15:51-56; Phil. 3:21). For those who endure and live godly lives, acknowledging and repenting immediately if sin occurs, you will inherit the kingdom (Ezek. 18:24-32; 1 Cor. 6:9-11;

Eph. 5:5-6; Gal. 5:19-21), be confident and unashamed (1 Jn. 2:28), and receive eternal riches and grace (Eph. 2:7; 3:11).

The purpose of the rapture is to also take the hinderer of lawlessness out of the world (2 Thess. 2:7-8), which is the church and is proved to be so in book two, *7 Rapture Views*, which gives the church saints at least seven years to live in heaven, to become familiar with the future life, and gear up for earth ruler-ship (Jn. 14:1-3; Dan. 9:27; Eph. 2:7; 3:11). How else would raptured saints know how to rule the earth except they go to be prepared in heaven?

Saints in heaven will eat and commune at the marriage supper of the Lamb. They will also travel back with Christ to earth to fight at Armageddon (Rev. 19; Zech. 14:1-5; Mat. 24:29-31; 2 Thess. 1:7-10; 2:7-8; Jude 14-15). How would saints who were just raptured turn right around in preparation for battle except they go and prepare? If there would be no rapture until the Second Coming, then all of these purposes would be canceled, as well as the fulfillment for all the promises to believers who overcome (Rev. 2:7, 11, 17, 26-27; 3:5, 11-12, 21; 2 Pt. 1:4; 2 Cor. 1:20). Let not the errors of many persuade you again that prophesy is not important to be a Christian. So many wrong gospels are taught for a lack of understanding. It's not that the Word isn't readily available, it's that it is not studied, much less harmonized.

Chapter 4

OUTLINING ALL RESURRECTIONS AND RAPTURES

Learning the many different kinds of raptures and resurrections can't be done on the run. You can't have the kids screaming at each other either. You really do need to concentrate. I know I always find a visual aid helpful, especially since I have ADHD pretty severely. The following pages outline the next two chapters (Chs. 5-6) in an easy to follow 4 outline series. Outline 1 will help you follow chapter 5. Outline 2 will guide you through chapter 6. Outlines 3-4 will be there for you when confusion covers you like a wet blanket from outlines 1-2. I'm just joking... These outlines, along with the very detailed chapters 5 and chapter 6 will make you an absolute pro at the subject of raptures and resurrections. You'll be teaching a class at church in no time!

OUTLINE 1

I. Resurrections
   A. Spiritual
      1. All People From Adam to the Last Man that Accepts Jesus to be Free From Sin
   B. Physical
      1. Natural Body
         a. Biblical Examples
            i. Elijah raised a woman's son
            ii. Elisha raised a woman's son
            iii. Jairus' Daughter
            iv. Lazarus
            v. A Widow's Son From Nain
            vi. Peter Raised Tabitha
            vii. Paul Raised a Young Man
         b. All Others Through Time Resurrected to Their Mortal Body
      2. Eternal Body
         a. The First Resurrection
            i. Jesus and the Many Saints Resurrected After His Resurrection
            ii. Everyone in Christ From Adam Till the End of the Church Age
            iii. The Tribulation Saints
            iv. The Two Witnesses
         b. The Second Resurrection
            i. The Antichrist and False Prophet
            ii. The Goats From the Judgment of the Nations
            iii. All People From Adam to the End of the Millennium
            iv. The Resurrection of the Giants

OUTLINE 2

I. Raptures
  A. Redeemed Man
    1. Soul and Spirit Only
      a. All Righteous Who Died Before Jesus Rose and Went to Abraham's Bosom
      b. All Righteous From Abraham's Bosom to Heaven
      c. All Righteous Who Have Died After Jesus Rose and Went to Heaven
      d. Every Person in Heaven at His Coming For the Saints Before the Tribulation
    2. Natural Body
      a. Enoch
      b. Elijah
      c. Moses
      d. Isaiah
      e. Philip
      f. Paul
      g. John
      h. Israel at the Second Coming
      i. People Found to be Sheep at the Judgment of Nations at the Second Coming
    3. Glorified and Eternal Body
      a. Jesus
      b. Many Old Testament Saints From Abraham's Bosom
      c. Every Person in Christ at His Coming For the Saints Before the Tribulation
      d. The 144,000 Jews in the Middle of the Tribulation
      e. The Tribulation Saints at the End of the

Tribulation
   f. The Two Witnesses at the End of the Tribulation
B. Condemned Man
   1. Soul and Spirit Only
      a. All Sinners and Unbelievers Who Will Ever Die and Go to Hell
      b. All Souls in Hell Brought to Their Body to be Brought to Judgment
   2. Natural Body
      a. People Found to be Goats at the Judgment of Nations at the Second Coming
   3. Eternal Body
      a. The Antichrist and the False Prophet
      b. Goats at the Judgment of Nations at the Second Coming Sent to Hell
      c. Natural People Who Rebel With Satan at the End of the Millennium
      d. Those in Hell to be Judged at the Time of the Great White Throne Judgment

OUTLINE 3

I. Rapture and Resurrection Combinations
   A. Redeemed Man
      1. Jesus and the Many Saints Resurrected After His Resurrection
      2. Spirits in Heaven at His Coming Before the Tribulation
      3. The Tribulation Saints at the End of the Tribulation
      4. The Two Witness' at the End of the Tribulation
   B. Condemned Man
      1. The Antichrist and False Prophet
      2. The Goats From the Judgment of the Nations
      3. All People From Adam to the End of the Millennium

Outline 3 groups all events that include a resurrection and a rapture together. You will notice this looks almost identical to outline 4, which is a visual list of the phases in both the first, and the second resurrection. The reason is there has never been and there never will be a resurrection from the dead resulting in a rapture that is not a part of the first or second resurrection. All resurrection / rapture combinations will still be future, except for Jesus' that began the first resurrection almost 2,000 years ago (1 Cor. 15:20-23).

OUTLINE 4

I. First and Second Resurrections
   A. First Resurrection (Redeemed Man)
      1. Jesus and the Many Saints Resurrected After His Resurrection
      2. Everyone in Christ, Dead or Alive, Before the Seven Year Tribulation
      3. The 144,000 Jews Caught Up in the Middle of the Tribulation
      4. The Tribulation Saints at the End of the Tribulation
      5. The Two Witnesses at the End of the Tribulation
   B. Second Resurrection (Condemned Man)
      1. The Antichrist and False Prophet at the Second Coming at the End of the Tribulation
      2. The Goats of the Judgment of the Nations Before the Beginning of the Millennium
      3. All People From Adam to the Last Rebel of God at the End of the Millennium

The first resurrection is a period of time lasting from Jesus' resurrection until the two witnesses resurrection and rapture at the end of the Tribulation. If the rapture is within the next few years, then the first resurrection's phases take place in the time span of about two thousand years. The second resurrection is a period of time lasting from the Antichrist and false prophet's resurrection and transportation to the lake of fire in hell at the Second Coming of Christ until hell is emptied from all the rest of the condemned souls at the end of the Millennial Reign for their resurrection and rapture to the Great White Throne Judgment in heaven. If the rapture is within the next few years, then the second resurrection's phases take place in the time span of about one thousand years.

Chapter 5

UNVEILING RESURRECTIONS THROUGH TIME

SPIRITUAL RESURRECTIONS

Biblically, there are two kinds of resurrections. First, being the resurrection of the spirit of man being made alive again from death in trespasses and sins. The spirit resurrection is a bringing of life to the spirit, not a coming into existence. The spirit resurrection can only happen in this life (Rom. 6:11; Eph. 2:1-6; 5:4). The man or woman who physically dies with a dead spirit enters eternal death with an everlasting existence in hell. They have no life because they are separated from the life source. That source of life is Jesus. He alone brings life. He is life (Jn. 14:6; 17:2-3; 1 Jn. 5:20). The condemned eternal soul is said to be dead because it is separated from life, not because is does not exist.

They will exist forever without the possibility of ever receiving Life again (Eccl. 11:1; Heb. 9:27; Rev. 20:11-15; 22:11). That's why committing your life and all your ways to God is so important in this age of profession and realm of testing. You only get one shot. God is giving all us free moral agents a little space in time to see if we will choose Him or not. The spiritual resurrection is the most important of the two and will be discussed in detail in chapter 7.

PHYSICAL RESURRECTIONS
NATURAL BODY
BIBLICAL EXAMPLES

The second kind of resurrection is a physical resurrection, which is the primary focus of this book. There are two kinds of physical resurrections: natural and eternal. Many natural resurrections have happened through time, even more than what's written in the Bible. Jesus told us that we can raise the dead as He did, so this shouldn't be a conflict (Mat. 10:8; 11:4-5; 28:18-20; Jn. 14:12). Scripture only records three people that Jesus raised from the dead: **Jairus' daughter** (Mat. 9:18-19, 23-25), **Lazarus** (Jn. 11:38-44), and a **widow's son from Nain** (Lk. 7:11-15). Aside from Jesus Christ, the Bible also records that Elijah, Elisha, Peter, and Paul raised the dead: **Elijah raised a woman's son** (1 Kings 17:17-24), **Elisha raised a woman's son** (2 Kings 4:17-37), **Peter raised Tabitha** (Acts 9:36-42), and **Paul raised a young man** (Acts 20:7-12).

Some would also include Jonah, though they are few. It just so happens that I agree. God did raise Jonah from the dead or else Jesus' words in Matthew 12:40 mean nothing.

> For as Jonas was three days and three nights in the whale's belly; so shall the Son of man be three days and three nights in the heart of the earth (Mat. 12:40).

Jonah was dead and was in the belly of the earth for three days and three nights or the reference to Jonah is worthless. Many teachers use every Old Testament character under the sun to use as a "type and shadow" of Christ, but Jonah was resurrected as a true type of Christ.

Jonah 2:1-2 tells us he was in the belly of the fish and in hell. Sheol is the Hebrew word for hell in that passage, and it does mean the place of departed souls. Before Jesus rose from the grave, all souls went to hell, though those accounted righteous had a safe chamber in the lower parts of the earth called paradise, or Abraham's Bosom (Lk. 16:19-31; 23:43). Jesus went to hell for three days to lead captivity captive (Eph. 4:8-10). Jonah was in Sheol after he died in the fish's belly and before he was resurrected.

> I went down to the bottoms of the mountains; the earth with her bars *was* about me for ever: yet hast thou brought up my life from corruption, O LORD my God. When my soul fainted within me I remembered the LORD: and my prayer came in unto thee, into thine holy temple.

Jonah prayed while in the belly of the fish before he died. He also prayed while in Sheol. There's more harmony in Scripture by the belief that Jonah was raised from the dead (Jonah 2:6-7).

I may not have all resurrections in the Bible presented here, but this should be adequate in dealing with the reality and perception of what defines a physical resurrection. Had I tried to list all resurrections, I might also mention Paul was most likely resurrected after being stoned. After all, he was so severely pelted with rocks that his executioners perceived him to be dead.

> And there came thither *certain* Jews from Antioch and Iconium, who persuaded the people, and, having stoned Paul, drew *him* out of the city, supposing he had been dead. Howbeit, as the disciples stood round about him, he <u>rose up</u>, and came into the city: and the next day he departed with Barnabas to Derbe (Acts 14:19-20).

The Greek word "anistemi" was translated "rose up," which means to stand up or rise again. It is used forty times of resurrection (Mat. 12:41; 17:9; 20:19; Mk. 8:31; 9:9, 31; 10:34; 12:23-26; Lk. 9:8, 19; 11:32; 16:31; 18:33; 24:7, 46; Jn. 6:39-40, 44, 54; 11:23-24; 20:9; Acts 2:24, 30, 32; 3:26; 10:41; 13:33-34; 14:20; 17:3, 31; Rom. 14:9; 15:12; Eph. 5:14; 1 Thess. 4:14, 16). The disciples stood around his body. You think maybe they might have been praying for Paul to be raised? I think so as well.

I know this concept was easy for you. The real confusion seems to be the rest of the story.

PHYSICAL RESURRECTIONS
NATURAL BODY
ALL OTHER EXAMPLES THROUGH TIME

For as the Father raises the dead and gives life to them, even so the Son gives life to whom He will (Jn. 5:21).

For He is not the God of the dead but of the living, for all live to Him (Lk. 20:38).

Why should it be thought incredible by you that God raises the dead (Acts 26:8)?

Yes, this is one of the two kinds of resurrections. Remember, there are two, spiritual and physical. We will be more specific when referring to the physical resurrections. Besides the specific examples given above, many people have been resurrected through time. All you have to do is google and you will find many such claims by way of NDE (near death experiences), and even visions. I suggest doing a search on, "Nigerian PASTOR Daniel Ekechukwu raised from dead." You'll see how serious it is to hold onto unforgiveness or sin, even as a believer who was saved.

PHYSICAL RESURRECTIONS
ETERNAL BODY
THE FIRST RESURRECTION

You just read of some natural resurrections, but the heart of the teaching of the resurrection for this book is that of the eternal resurrection. There are two kinds of eternal resurrections: the first resurrection and the second resurrection. The first eternal resurrection is of all the righteous who have physically died from Adam's day to the end of the 7 Year Tribulation. The 7 Year Tribulation ends because Jesus and all resurrected saints physically come back from heaven to rule and reign the earth for one thousand years (Rev. 20: 2-7). This period is one of an infinite amount of thousand year periods that will be ruled by Jesus and His saints (Dan. 7:18).

This first thousand-year reign is called the Millennial Reign; it is another doctrinal term. The second eternal resurrection is that of all the wicked, unbelieving, and / or sinful (Mat. 25:31-46; Rev. 21:8). This resurrection has three parts beginning with the Antichrist and False Prophet, followed by the goats in the judgment of the nations, and then those innumerable who have been in hell awaiting the Great White Throne Judgment (Rev. 20:11-15; Jn. 5:28-29).

Now, as for all analytical thinkers who are doing the math, you have already seen a hole in the story, so you think. You may wonder how the first eternal resurrection (only the righteous) is said to be completed at the end of the Tribulation period when the Bible teaches a pre-tribulation rapture (proven in book 2). Wouldn't that mean the first resurrection ends before the Tribulation begins?

The fact is that there are five phases, or parts, in the first resurrection. Very few have ever heard this teaching. This is no surprise. Seldom is the rapture of the church even taught in rapture believing churches. Many are the churches who mention it and say it is soon, while never actually teaching the doctrine even partially, much less in its entirety. The five phases will be taught thoroughly in chapters 5 - 6.

As you remember from outline 1, I showed the phases, or parts, to the first resurrection, but only four were given since they include a resurrection. There are actually five phases in the first resurrection and all five phases include a rapture, or a catching up of saints to heaven (outline 4). This will be the introduction of the four eternal resurrections of the first resurrection. I'll acquaint you with this now, followed by the second resurrection, which also consists of some phases. Three to be exact.

The next chapter is what has stimulated the minds of the watchers since Paul revealed this mystery to the 1st century church. It will be time to introduce the rapture and then go way beyond introduction to intimate relationship. I know you'll fall in love with this doctrine if you are not already there. Refresh your memory with outline 2 before venturing on to that chapter (Ch. 6). It shows all past, present, and future raptures as we did with the resurrection outline. Through all the outlines and pages, we will unravel all the details in a detailed thorough study. This will all make perfect sense when all the puzzle pieces are brought to the table to show the clear picture. The harmony of it all will be edifying. Never again will you be shaken by the rapture / resurrection doctrine.

Unveiling Resurrections Through Time

THE FIRST RESURRECTION JESUS AND THE MANY SAINTS RESURRECTED AFTER HIS RESURRECTION

As stated previously, the first resurrection consists of five parts. Only four are resurrections, so this is what we'll wrestle with at the moment. Jesus is the first fruits of the resurrection (1 Cor. 15:20, 23). Without further ado, let's talk about the author and finisher of our faith. He is the reason and purpose I was able to write this book, and He is the hope I am sharing to give faith to the seeker, and to embolden the expectancy of the believer.

> But now is Christ risen from the dead, *and* become the firstfruits of them that slept. For since by man *came* death, by man *came* also the resurrection of the dead. For as in Adam all die, even so in Christ shall all be made alive. But every man in his own order: Christ the firstfruits; afterward they that are Christ's at his coming (1 Cor. 15:20-23).

[firstfruits] Greek: *aparche* (GSN-<G536>), firstfruits; the beginning of a thing. In this case it means that Jesus is the first of the dead to be resurrected into the immortal body. Jesus' resurrection is not the first resurrection ever as we have seen, but His is the first resurrection where the body is changed to its eternal condition. Unlike the resurrections of people from Old Testament prophets and during Jesus' ministry on earth, His soul and spirit will never again be separated from His body in a future death as is what takes place in a natural resurrection.

Another distinction must be made regarding the rapture of Enoch and Elijah. They are not the first to be resurrected and taken to heaven as many have assumed. If they were resurrected, or even changed to their immortal body as Jesus, then Jesus would not be the first fruits of the dead as is taught in Scripture (1 Cor.15:20, 23). Instead, Enoch would have been the first fruits of the resurrection about 3,500 years before Jesus.

Enoch and Elijah were taken to heaven in natural bodies and will be the two witnesses of Revelation 11 and Zechariah 4. We will go further into that on later pages. The fact is that Jesus is the first to be transformed from having a natural body to having an eternal, immortal body. I would say "glorified body" and this would be accurate, but the truth is that even the unrighteous will receive an immortal body, yet theirs is not glorified (Rev. 20:4-6, 11-15).

Jesus is only the first of the first part of the first resurrection (Keep referring to chapter 4, outline 4, and this will all be clear with practice... I know it's confusing at first). The rest of the resurrected were many Old Testament saints who were resurrected after Jesus' resurrection (1 Cor. 15:20, 23; Mat. 27:52-53; Eph. 4:8-10). Jesus came to earth to set the unrighteous free by living a perfect life so that our sins could be taken away, not merely covered (Jn. 3:15-21; 8:31-36; 1 Jn. 3:1-7).

Before Jesus rose in victory over death, hell and the grave, all righteous went to a place in the earth called Abraham's Bosom, or paradise (Lk. 16:22; 23:43). That was one of five chambers in hell. Those saved people in the earth were being held captive by Satan because he had legal right to them since their sins were not yet taken away, only covered. They were, like Abraham, account righteous (Gen. 15:6; Rom. 4:3-5; Gal. 3:6; Jas. 2:23). No harm came to them since they were saved. Nevertheless, they were awaiting the future first coming of the Messiah like the faithful children of God today are awaiting the second coming of the Lord at the trumpet sound (1 Thess. 4:16-17; 1 Cor. 15:51-54; Rev. 4:1).

If this is new to you then definitely open your Bible, or Bible online for free, and look up these verses (2 Tim. 2:15). Adam was the first man, and because of his fall from righteousness (Gen. 2:17; 3:1-19), there came the spiritual death penalty of sin, which resulted in physical death (1 Cor. 15:21-22).. These deaths passed upon all people (Rom. 5:12-21). Thus, the very reason you are even reading about a future resurrection now.

It wasn't supposed to be this way. This is not the way God intended it to be. Instead of living forever by remaining sinless and eating from the Tree of Life, the body must be resurrected in the future resurrection of the dead (1 Cor. 15:35-54; Dan. 12:2; Jn. 5:28-29). The only time spiritual and eternal deaths can be called off, resurrecting one from death in trespasses and sin, is in this life (Eph. 2:1-9; 1 Jn. 1:9). After death comes the judgment without any chance to be saved, if one dies unsaved (Heb. 9:27; Rev. 20:11-15; 21:8; 22:11).

Jesus accomplished one of His earthly missions when He entered into the lower parts of the earth, but unlike any man before or ever after Him, He lived a sinless life (2 Cor. 5:21; Heb. 4:15; 1 Pt. 2:21-22; 1 Jn. 3:5) and went into hell to conquer it and release imprisoned souls from Satan (Eph. 4:8-10; Ps. 16:10; 68:18; Mt. 12:40; Heb. 2:14-15)

> Wherefore he saith, When he ascended up on high, he led captivity captive, and gave gifts unto men. (Now that he ascended, what is it but that <u>he also descended first into the lower parts of the earth</u>? He that descended is the same also that ascended up far above all heavens, that he might fill all things) (Eph. 4:8-10).

So, in wrapping up the first part of the first resurrection that began almost two thousand years ago, Jesus went to the lower parts of the earth and He took those captives captive to heaven. But something happened between Jesus going into the lower parts of earth and taking the righteous souls to heaven.

> And the graves were opened; and many bodies of the saints which slept arose, And came out of the graves after his resurrection, <u>and went into the holy city, and appeared unto many</u> (Mat. 27:52-53).

As you see, those Old Testament saints that bodily rose after Jesus did (since He is the first fruits of the resurrection – 1 Cor. 15:20, 23), went walking around for a bit and appeared to many as a witness to the truth of Jesus.

The time when Jesus led those bodily risen souls to heaven was at the ascension, 40 days after His resurrection (Acts 1:3-11; Lk. 24:51; Mk. 16:19). All the righteous taken from Abraham's Bosom (paradise), in the lower parts of the earth, were taken to heaven at the time of the ascension, but the "many" from Matthew 27:52-53 were the bodily resurrected saints. The rest were the immortal souls that were not resurrected, but were liberated from captivity to Satan (Heb. 2:14-15; 12:23). Not all were resurrected back to their body, but all were translated from paradise to earth, and then from earth to heaven 40 days later. By definition, those were raptures, but we won't dive into that until the next chapter, after we go over all resurrections.

Unveiling Resurrections Through Time

THE FIRST RESURRECTION EVERYONE IN CHRIST FROM ADAM TILL THE END OF THE CHURCH AGE

The next part in the first resurrection is the most familiar to the masses. Even those who are accounted with the unbelievers have heard of this event. Yes, the phrase that gives me goosebumps and brings a twinkle to my eyes every time I hear it, "The rapture of the church!" Technically, there is only one resurrection in this second phase of the first resurrection, and it is not the church people who are alive at the coming of the Lord with the splendor of that notorious trumpet sound (1 Cor. 15:52; 1 Thess. 4:16). Just hold tight a little longer and all these rapture and resurrection phases will be brought together!

First, the resurrections. Let's talk about those immortal souls that were not resurrected bodily at the resurrection of Jesus with many Old Testament saints. They were merely liberated from captivity to Satan (Heb. 2:14-15; 12:23) and are now about to receive their resurrection of their immortal souls joined together with their mortal bodies. They will finally be risen and glorified to immortality and incorruptibly for all eternity. Honestly, I'm not certain as to why some righteous were resurrected to their immortal state with Jesus, while others were just taken to heaven and still await their resurrection with the church. The Bible never gives a reason.

We can only speculate, because we do know not all the righteous in Abraham's Bosom were bodily resurrected. They were raptured without a resurrection at that time. My speculation is that the resurrection of Jesus was so great an event that all the bodies of the righteous dead within a certain radius of the tomb of Jesus were raised to life. My speculation is based on the fact that many people in that area were reported to have seen the many (Mat. 27:52-53). The entire earth had dead bodies buried within, since man had been living and dying for 4,000 years at that time. Others around the world may have been resurrected to immortality, but we just don't have all those details.

Regardless, now is their time to shine with all those in Christ who have died after the resurrection of Christ almost two thousand years ago. All these physically dead Old Testament and New Testament saints from Adam's day until the trumpet sound will have part in this resurrection. Those of us who are alive and in Christ will join them and be changed also into immortality and incorruptibility, but will not technically be resurrected since we never died. The time in which this happens will be before the beginning of the Tribulation, before the apostasy, before the revealing of Antichrist, and before the great deception (2 Thess. 2:1-12). Refer to book 2, *7 Rapture Views*.

New facts learned are hard to keep organized until they're embedded in our understanding. To refocus, the "rapture of the church" is this second phase of the first resurrection. (Trying to keep your mind untangled). This will consist of the church (making up all dead and alive saints from the beginning of the church age until that moment) and the Old Testament saints who were not physically resurrected when Jesus was resurrected (1 Thess. 4:16-17).

I assure you that the saints in heaven are just as filled with anticipation for the rapture event and their resurrection as we are down here who are faithfully watching for the return of the Lord in the air to receive us to Himself. All best days of a person's life combined will be lingering in the shadow of the splendor and experience of that moment in time.

All your loved ones in heaven will meet you in the air. Any child aborted, miscarried, or otherwise in heaven is eagerly anticipating that day to see you face to face and cheering you on in this life, because they don't want you to miss the mark, fall from the race, lose this war, or be disqualified from the prize of eternal life for those who endure until the end (Phil. 3:14; Mat. 10:22-28; Lk. 9:59-62; 1 Cor. 9:24-27; Heb. 4:1, 11). I know I have three siblings in heaven that I look forward to hugging in the moments directly after the resurrection of all dead in Christ, and the rapture of all in Christ, dead and alive.

If you have unforgiveness, hate, unbelief, or sin in your life, please for the love of the one who gave you life, repent and get ready to meet your Glorious God in the sky with all the saints in heaven. If you have been guilty of abortion, forgive yourself and know that your child loves you and can't wait to be held in your arms, even if they have been raised to adulthood in heaven. It may be helpful to have a good cry and to pray to Jesus, not ever the dead (Lev. 20:27; Dt. 18:10-13). Ask Him to tell those children that you love them and you are so sorry. I believe this is allowed and crucial to the healing process, because dying with unforgiveness damns your soul for eternity and your portion will be in the lake of fire consigned to all the damned at the second resurrection (Mat. 6:12-15; 18:21-35; Mk. 11:25-26; Rev. 21:8).

FIRST RESURRECTION
THE 144,000 / MAN CHILD

The third part of the first resurrection has no resurrection at all, because those 144,000 making up this phase in the first resurrection are alive during the first half, or 3 ½ years of the Seven Year Tribulation. They are so alive that they have even been given a seal on their foreheads so they can all be protected from the trumpet judgments of Revelation (Rev. 7:1-3; 9:4).

You might wonder how this company can be a part of the resurrection if they have never died. I say this is just as simple as it was to include the saints who never died in the rapture of the church 3 ½ years prior to the catching up of this company of saints. Both are alive at the time of their glorious change to put on immortality. Neither group had ever tasted death, just as the prophet Paul had proclaimed (1 Cor.15:51-54). This was one of Paul's revelations.

Even though it has been appointed for everyone to die once (Heb.9:27), the ones alive at the second and third phase of the first resurrection will not physically die, because some will be changed to the likeness of those who do die (1 Thess. 4:13-17). This is part of the plan of God for man that sums up the last dispensation where natural man rules this earth. All these glorified saints will in fact be the ones to rule and reign with Christ, even ruling over the angels and all eternal generations of man (Ps. 149:6-9; Dan. 7:18, 27; Lk. 22:30; Rom. 8:17; 1 Cor. 6:2-4; 2 Tim. 2:12; Heb. 12:28; Rev. 1:6; 2:26-27; 3:21; 5:10; 12:5; 20:4-6; 22:4-5). Proof of the rapture and eternal glorification of the 144,000 (Rev. 7:1-8; 14:1-5) to be the third part of the first resurrection will be proven later. But we must touch slightly on the "why" of these resurrections. I'll begin by stating it has always been a sad fact to know that hell is overwhelmingly more populated with humans than heaven is (Mat. 7:13-14; Lk. 13:24-27).

The good news for all living is that no one has to go to hell, and because of the dispensations of God for man in this age of testing, there will come a dispensation soon that begins the Dispensation of Divine Government, where all people will be in two classes: glorified man and natural man. All who have part in this first resurrection will be the glorified saints that rule the entire universe (Ps. 8; Isa. 45:18; 66:22-24; Rev. 21- Rev. 22), while natural man are those who were permitted to enter into the Millennial Reign and all their offspring, and their offspring's offspring, for eternal generations (Mat. 25:31-46). At some point during that time there will be a break even point for souls in hell verses souls on earth. From that point on the righteous souls of man will continuously grow to outnumber those in the lake of fire. Some have said hell is winning, but that is only a matter of perspective and knowledge of the future as given from Scripture.

THE FIRST RESURRECTION
THE TRIBULATION SAINTS

Part four of this first resurrection is one hardly ever thought about, and quite frankly never taught to me by any pastor I've ever sat under. The lack of knowledge and understanding on end-times is astounding. But we were all born without any of our learning in all fields of study and development. We must be patient and apt to teach what we learn so that a few will believe and receive. Even Jesus had to learn Scripture. This is because He emptied Himself of all divine knowledge when He came to earth as a baby (Isa. 7:14-16; 11:2; 50:4-11; 53:1-12; Lk. 2:40, 52; Phil. 2:6-8; Heb. 2:14-18; 5:8-9). So be encouraged, don't feel beat up! Get excited about learning all the facets of the rapture doctrine!

This resurrection will be a no brainer to you after you read one passage and think about it for a moment. Don't all the martyred saints rule and reign with Christ?

And I saw thrones, and they sat upon them, and judgment was given unto them: and *I saw* the souls of them that were beheaded for the witness of Jesus, and for the word of God, and which had not worshipped the beast, neither his image, neither had received *his* mark upon their foreheads, or in their hands; and they lived and reigned with Christ a thousand years. But the rest of the dead lived not again until the thousand years were finished. This *is* the first resurrection. Blessed and holy *is* he that hath part in the first resurrection: on such the second death hath no power, but they shall be priests of God and of Christ, and shall reign with him a thousand years (Rev. 20:4-6).

Will there ever be a people that rule and reign on earth with Christ for a thousand years and then on into eternity on the New Earth who are not resurrected? Truth is, most couldn't answer that with certainty, but I tell you no. All who die and are in heaven at any point will be raised and rule in a glorified body.

These "tribulation saints" are a group of people that have become saved after the rapture of the church. To be clear, some may have been believers at the time of the rapture, but were caught sleeping, living in sin, and had not heeded the command and warning to remain in Christ and endure until the end so their crown would not be taken from them (Mat. 10:22-28; Jn. 15:1-6, 15; 1 Cor. 9:24-27; 15:2, 33-34; Gal. 1:6-9; 2:21; Heb. 4:1, 11; Rev. 3:11; chapter 8). They are present on earth after the church age has ended and will become a separate group from the church itself (Rev. 6:9-11; 7:9-17; 13:7; 14:12-13; 15:1-4; 17:7; 20:1-6).

Some say this group is saved, being called saints, therefore is part of the church, or the church itself. They use this as proof against a pre-tribulation rapture (Dan. 7:21). The truth is that this company of believers are all saints, but not the church at all. This can be easily perceived by acknowledging there have been many saints of old who are not part of the church.

Old Testament saints are not part of the church, whether saved before the law of Moses or after it, regardless of national ties with Israel or not (Jonah 3:4-10). The church has it's space in time beginning during Jesus' ministry and ending at the trumpet sound of the second part of the first resurrection (Mat. 10; 16:18; Lk. 16:16; Acts 1:15-26; Eph. 1:21-23; 1 Thess. 4:13-17; Rev. 4:1).

Some say the church will be here during the tribulation because the gospel will be preached throughout this period.

> And this gospel of the kingdom shall be preached in all the world for a witness unto all nations; and then shall the end come (Mat. 24:14).

But can't this be easily accounted for by the fact that people will believe the gospel by the burden of proof of all the righteous being taken off the earth? Does the church alone know the gospel? Don't the wicked, unbelieving, and sinners of all kind know the gospel? How many unsaved people are there around you daily who have heard of Jesus and rejected Him?

Yes, we can all be honest with ourselves and simply acknowledge this truth even if you do not believe a professing Christian in sin will be left behind. The truth is that those who will preach the gospel during the Seven Year Tribulation will not be a part of the Church. They are people who have missed the rapture of the glorious church (Eph. 5:27; 1 Jn. 2:28 – 3:3). They will become saved and preach to others during the Tribulation period. Aside from these tribulation saints, the gospel will also be proclaimed by the 144,000 Jews

(Rev. 7:1-8), the two witnesses (Rev. 11:3-13; Zech. 4:11-14; Mal. 4:5-6), and also three angels (Rev. 14:6-12).

The great multitude of tribulation saints who are saved after the rapture of the church (Rev. 4:1) will all die or be killed sometime between Revelation 6:1 – 19:10. The first martyrs (people killed for their faith) of this period are told to rest until the remainder of them are killed (Rev. 6:9-11). These first martyrs will be killed by the great whore of Revelation 17:1-7. They will be martyred between the rapture and the 5th seal in the first 3 1/2 years of the tribulation.

The great whore is a religious system who rules the ten kingdoms of the old Roman Empire territory until the beginning of the Great Tribulation (the halfway point of the 7 Year Tribulation), then the Antichrist takes over the entire kingdom and establishes beast worship, destroying the great whore (Rev. 13, 17). This system is most likely Islam since we can all see the influx of Muslim immigrants bringing domination that's resculpting the land now. Catholicism also fits the biblical criteria for exposing the identity of the whore.

The rest of the martyred saints are killed by the beast, or Antichrist, in the last three and a half years (Rev. 7:9-17; 13:7; 14:12-13; 15:1-4; 17:7; 20:1-6), then retribution will be given as cried out for by the first martyred saints of that time. These saints were told to wait until all who were to be martyred in the tribulation would be killed, and then their death would be avenged (Rev. 6:9-11). All the righteous dead will be raptured in time for the marriage supper of the Lamb (Rev. 19:1-10) to ride back to earth with Christ. At that time all resurrected saints take back the world from the enemies of God (Rev. 19:11-16).

The time of the resurrection of these Tribulation saints is after the destruction of literal Babylon (Rev. 18), which is at the very end of the seven-year period and right before the marriage supper in heaven. The marriage supper takes place immediately before the Second Coming (Rev. 19:1-16).

> And <u>after these things</u> I heard a great voice of <u>much people in heaven</u>, saying, Alleluia; Salvation, and glory, and honour, and power, unto the Lord our God: For true and righteous *are* his judgments: for he hath judged the great whore, which did corrupt the earth with her fornication, and <u>hath avenged the blood of his servants</u> at her hand. And again they said, Alleluia. And her smoke rose up for ever and ever. And <u>the four and twenty elders and the four beasts fell down and worshipped God</u> that sat on the throne, saying, Amen; Alleluia (Rev. 19:1-4).

So, after the destruction of Babylon (which we will learn all about in book 3 of the *Millions Vanished Series*), many people are in heaven, proving they have been caught up in time for the marriage of the Lamb.

Many will claim there is only one rapture and resurrection, which is at the Second Coming when Jesus comes back with His saints (Zech. 14:5; Jude 14-15; Rev. 19:14). They believe there is no rapture of saints to heaven, believing also that the marriage supper of the Lamb will be held in the air at the time Christ raptures the saints (Eph. 5:27; Col. 3:4; 1 Thess. 3:13; 4:16-17; 2 Thess. 2:7-8; Rev. 4:1). This is called the yo-yo rapture – up and right back down.

As you have clearly seen above in Revelation 19:1, there are many people in heaven, and at that time these many people are eating and about to mount up on their warrior horses to ride through a portal from heaven to earth (Rev. 4:1; 19:11). I also underlined "hath avenged the blood of his servants" (Rev. 19:2) to show that the request from the first set of tribulation saints has been fulfilled (Rev. 6:9-11), which sought vengeance to those who shed their blood. In keeping with the order of Revelation 4 – Revelation 5, the twenty-four elders and the four beasts are seen again worshiping God after a resurrection and rapture (Rev. 4:1). All future tribulation saints will be resurrected to their immortal and incorruptible body right before the ride from heaven to earth (Zech. 14:5; Jude 14-15; Rev. 19:11-16).

THE FIRST RESURRECTION
THE TWO WITNESSES

The resurrection of the two witnesses ends the first resurrection that began with the resurrection of Christ (Mat. 27:52-53; 1 Cor. 15:20, 23; Eph. 4:8-10; Rev. 11:7-11). I had a friend once confess to me that he wondered if he would be one of those two witnesses. Sounds funny now, maybe even egotistical, but his intentions were nothing of the sort. At the time, he was very young in knowledge and understanding and was more hoping he would be one, rather than thinking he deserves to be one. The two witnesses are none other than Enoch and Elijah. They have never tasted death, nor have these two been resurrected, yet they have both been in the presence of God day and night for thousands of years each (Zech. 4:11-14).

Enoch lived before the world-wide flood of Noah, some 4 ½ thousand years ago. He was seventh from Adam and walked with God in the same sense that Adam walked with God in the garden. He had his son at sixty-five years old, named Methuselah. He then walked with God for three hundred years until he was caught up in his natural body to be with the Lord until his mission on earth to be one of Christ's two witnesses at the end of our dispensation (Gen. 2:19; 3:8; 5:21-24).

Enoch was one of Christ's witnesses even from his days before the flood. He had written a book of the many things God revealed to him and allowed him to see. Without going further into that, we know that Enoch prophesied of the Second Coming, which was at a point in time over three thousand years before the First Coming of Christ happened (Enoch 1:9; Jude 14-15). Though none of us can be one of the two witnesses, we can all be a witness for Christ by proclaiming the good news of the gospel and all future events to come so people can get ready and stay ready (Mat. 25:1-13; Mk. 13:34-37; Lk. 21:34-36; Rev. 3:11)!

Many people believe it to be problematic to conceive of two natural bodied men in heaven all these thousands of years, but to God this is nothing. Weren't John and Paul both taken to heaven to see things revealed to them in heaven (2 Cor. 12:1-7; Rev. 4:1)? If you can conceive two men in natural bodies being in heaven for a few minutes, then why not a few thousand years? Is God not beyond space and time? Is time Lord over God? No way!

Some say sinful flesh cannot be in the presence of God, no sin at all for that matter, but I bring forth the evidence of Satan, father of all sin, going to the throne of God for many thousands of years to accuse the saints (Job 1:6 – 2:7; Rev. 12:10). We can see from the prophet Zechariah that there are two anointed men who stand by the God of the earth until they are to go back to earth and fulfill their mission from God (Rev. 11:3-11).

> Then answered I, and said unto him, What *are* these two olive trees upon the right *side* of the candlestick and upon the left *side* thereof? And I answered again, and said unto him, What *be these* two olive branches which through the two golden pipes empty the golden *oil* out of themselves?

And he answered me and said, Knowest thou not what these *be*? And I said, No, my lord. Then said he, These *are* the two anointed ones, that stand by the Lord of the whole earth (Zech. 4:11-14).

The short story of Enoch tells all we need to know about how to be right with God so we can have part in the first resurrection of the righteous.

By faith Enoch <u>was translated that he should not see death</u>; and was not found, because God had translated him: for before his translation he had this testimony, that <u>he pleased God</u>. But <u>without faith *it is* impossible to please *him*</u>: for he that cometh to God <u>must believe that he is</u>, and *that* he is a rewarder of them that <u>diligently seek him</u> (Heb.11:5-6; cpl w/ Rom. 10:17).

We must believe God and seek Him, not just once, but continually through life (Dan. 12:2; Mat. 7:13-14; 10:22; 19:28-29; 25:46; Mk. 10:29-30; Lk. 18:29-30; Rom. 2:7; 5:21; 6:21-23; Gal. 6:7-8; Heb. 3:6, 12-14; 6:11-12; 10:23, 35-39; 1 Tim. 1:16; 4:8; 6:12, 19; Tit. 1:2; 3:7; 1 Pt. 1:5, 9, 13; 3:7; 1 Jn. 2:25; Jude 20-24; Rev. 2:7, 11, 17, 26; 3:5, 12, 21).

Another proof of Enoch's rapture to heaven without death has been underlined in that passage above. "...Enoch <u>was translated that he should not see death</u>..." (Heb. 11:5). Some have pointed this out as proof against him being one of the two witnesses because verse 5 states that Enoch should not see death. Seems logical, after all, both the two witnesses will die before they are resurrected and caught up to heaven again (Gen. 5:21-24; 2 Kings 2; Rev. 11:7-12).

But Enoch's death had merely not been appointed for that time, because he was going to fulfill a great purpose for the testimony of Jesus and be a great defender of Israel against

Antichrist during the last 3 ½ years of this age. He will have his appointed time to die, it was just not appointed for him during his time before the flood.

> And as it is appointed unto men once to die, but after this the judgment (Heb. 9:27).

The second witness is Elijah. This is in little dispute among those who agree that these two witnesses are men, and not covenants, dispensations, angels, or anything else. Malachi foretells Elijah's return before the Day of the Lord. The Second Coming until the last day of the Millennial Reign is for him every Passover.

> Behold, I will send you Elijah the prophet before the coming of the great and dreadful day of the LORD: And he shall turn the heart of the fathers to the children, and the heart of the children to their fathers, lest I come and smite the earth with a curse (Mal. 4:5-6).

The day of the Lord is a doctrine we will thoroughly go over in book three, *The Watcher's Guide*. So, before the day of the Lord, Elijah will physically come back. Even religious Jews accept this and look for him every Passover.

Elijah and Enoch are the only two men to never taste death from prior generations. They will be allowed to be killed at the end of their ministry, which is for 1,260 days, or 3 ½ years. After they are killed, their bodies will lay in the streets for 3 ½ days before God brings their souls back to those bodies and raises them to their immortal condition forever. After that, a great voice from heaven will say, "Come up hither," and they will then ascend up to heaven (Rev. 11:7-12). Remember, Jesus is the first fruits of the Resurrection, so neither Enoch nor Elijah were taken to heaven in a glorified body during their first raptures into heaven (Gen. 5:21-24; 2 Ki. 2). They did not die in those days, so their physical, eternal resurrection will take place at the end of the future tribulation period.

PHYSICAL RESURRECTIONS
ETERNAL BODY
SECOND RESURRECTION

The second resurrection has three parts. This will be easily understood now that you have learned of the many phases a resurrection can have. The second resurrection is for the damned only. This includes the condemned souls of all people, beginning with Adam and ending with the last person who chooses to rebel against God at the end of the Millennial Reign. They will all be raised to immortality of the body in the second resurrection. As in the case with the righteous, all unrighteous souls have never ceased to exist and will always remain in a conscious state of awareness, despite the ungodly belief that the soul of the dead are asleep. This is known as soul-sleep, or annihilationism.

The souls in hell will one day reunite with their bodies and be immortal, though their bodies will constantly be in anguish by the eternal destruction of the fire in hell (Rev. 21:8). The horrific nightmare motivating me to speak unpopular truth is the people tormented in hell will never die (Isa. 66:22-24; Rev. 14:9-11). This disproves that only the righteous will put on immortality. The truth is that only the righteous will put on incorruptibility (1 Cor. 15:51-54), but all will be immortal (Rev. 20:11-15).

Unveiling Resurrections Through Time

SECOND RESURRECTION THE ANTICHRIST AND THE FALSE PROPHET

The first part, or phase, of this resurrection from among the damned are the two infamous agents of the apocalypse: the Antichrist and his false prophet. At the Second Coming, these two will stand against Jesus and His army. They will be killed by Christ, Himself (Rev. 19:11-21).

> And I saw the beast was taken, and with him the false prophet that wrought miracles before him, with which he deceived them that had received the mark of the beast, and them that worshipped his image. These both were cast alive into a lake of fire burning with brimstone (Rev. 19:19-20).

As we have already discussed, the remainder of all the damned will be resurrected at the end of the Millennial Reign. The second resurrection takes at least one thousand years to complete. Just like the first resurrection that will take around two thousand years to complete, there are a few phases that extend the resurrections beyond a one-day time frame as many believe it to be. The first resurrection, consisting of only the righteous, began with the resurrection of Christ. In like manner, the second resurrection, consisting of only the unrighteous, begins with the resurrection of Antichrist.

If you've noticed, the first resurrection is completely finished before the beginning of the second resurrection. Since the two witnesses ended the resurrection of the just, we can conclude that the separation of time between the two different resurrections is only a short time consisting of at least four days. The two witnesses will be killed at the end of the Tribulation. The Antichrist and false prophet will be killed at the Second Coming. The two witnesses will be dead in the streets for 3.5 days, then resurrected and raptured to heaven to take part in the marriage supper of the Lamb.

After that, Jesus, the holy angels, and all His saints in heaven will fly through that opened portal and conquer the Antichrist, the false prophet, and all his army at the Second Coming. This time span clue of "at least four days" is an exciting revelation found in book three, *The Watcher's Guide* (Mark 13:34-37).

One more nugget revealed on the timeline can be seen above when I made the statement that the second resurrection will be "at least" 1,000 years in duration. Well, we know the beginning of the second resurrection is at the Second Coming, and we know that the thousand years begins after that. We know the end of this resurrection happens after the thousand years are over. What many don't catch is that Satan is bound for 1,000 years, and then is released for a short time in order to gather a great multitude of the subjects of the kingdom, the natural people, so he can lead one last attempt in battling against God, His angels, and all His glorified and natural people who have not chosen to follow that outstanding terminal rebellion (Rev. 20:1-10).

> And I saw an angel come down from heaven, having the key of the bottomless pit and a great chain in his hand. And he laid hold on the dragon, that old serpent, which is the Devil, and Satan, and bound him a thousand years, And cast him into the bottomless pit, and shut him up, and set a seal upon him, that he should deceive the nations no more, <u>till the thousand years should be fulfilled</u>: and after that he must be loosed <u>a little season</u> (Rev. 20:1-3).

So the thousand years must come to a full completion, or be fulfilled, before Satan has his little piece of time to build an army. If the little season here is the same as the short time (Rev. 12:12) and the short space (Rev. 17:10), it will be only 3 ½ years (Rev. 12:12-14; 13:5). If this is the case, then the second resurrection will last 1,003 ½ years. All kinds of pieces are brought together in book 3 that go way beyond those nuggets of gold that all watchers are hungry for. You don't want to miss it!

Back to the first phase of the second resurrection. A quick reading of the destruction of the Antichrist and his false prophet may look as if they were not resurrected, merely raptured (translated from one place to another) to hell's fires. After all, the end of Revelation 19:20 says, "…These both were cast alive into a lake of fire burning with brimstone." Doesn't it almost sound like they had no resurrection at all?

I would agree that it does sound that way, but we must harmonize all scripture on a subject to get the full meaning. After all, it would appear that all the gathered armies at Armageddon are destroyed by the sword from Jesus' mouth if we just read Revelation 19:15. But the truth is that only five out of six are killed (Ezek. 39:2), and Christ is not the only one doing the killing. The army of the Antichrist is also destroyed by angels (2 Thess. 1:7-10), saints (Rev. 19:14; Jude 1:14; Zech. 14:5), a cloudburst (Ezek. 38:22), great hailstones (Rev. 16:21; Ezek. 38:22), fire and brimstone (Ezek. 38:22), pestilence and blood (Ezek. 38:22), the Jewish army of natural men (Zech. 14:14), and by self-destruction (Zech. 14:13).

> I beheld then because of the voice of the great words which the horn spake: I beheld *even* till the beast was slain, and his body destroyed, and given to the burning flame (Dan. 7:11).

The word destroyed means they will be killed, not cease to exist. The Antichrist and false prophet will be two mortal men killed at Armageddon (2 Thess. 2:7-8). It is appointed for everyone to die once (Heb. 9:27), so they are mortal men, not resurrected men from the past who have already died, nor is the Antichrist Satan incarnate.

Satan will be bound and cast into hell with the Antichrist and false prophet as a distinct and different being (Rev. 20:1-3, 10). Their bodies will be resurrected and cast into eternal hell (Dan. 7:11; Rev. 19:20; 20:10). They are slain, resurrected immediately into their immortal bodies, and then cast alive into the lake of fire. They will not be resurrected for the Great White Throne Judgment, because they are immediately judged by Jesus for their rebellion against the living God.

THE SECOND RESURRECTION THE GOATS FROM THE JUDGMENT OF THE NATIONS

The Judgment of the Nations takes place after the Second Coming and right before the Millennial Reign of Christ and His saints. There will be a gap of time of a few days between the Second Coming and the Millennial Reign as we shall see in book three, but what this does for us now is to show the order of the second resurrection. The gentile nations are the ones that have part in this judgment. These people are specific to one generation, the last people alive at the coming of Jesus (Mat. 25:32). The odds of surviving the Seven Year Tribulation are not great, not even a little. So this group has seen and been through a lot.

Some will be guilty, while others will be free to enter into life under perfect rule. It will not be every person in all nations, for many will not know Jesus has even come back from heaven. Evangelizing will continue, because the gospel of the kingdom shall be preached in all the world, not every individual in every nation, for many will not have heard the good news until the Millennium (Isa. 2; 66:19-21; Zech. 8:23). The judgment of these sheep and goats will be an individual judgment of all participating with Israel when Christ comes to set up His kingdom.

The foundation of their judgment is based on their treatment of Christ's brethren, the Jews (Mat. 25:31-46). Some will be saved to go into the Millennium. They are the sheep. Some will be destroyed by being made immortal and cast into the lake of fire for eternity (Mat. 13:41-50; 24:51; 25:34, 41, 46; Zech. 14; Isa. 53; Joel 3). They are the goats (Mat. 25:41, 46), and like the rapture of the church who are alive at the trumpet sound, and like the 144,000, the goats will not be killed.

Therefore, they will not be resurrected, even though they will make up one phase of many in the second resurrection. They will simply be changed and transported from earth to the lake of fire with no hope of redemption and no resurrection at the end of the Millennium. They will accompany Satan, the Antichrist, and the false prophet in fire for the duration of at least one thousand years, until the rest of the wicked dead are resurrected, judged, and cast to the lake of fire with them (Rev. 20).

SECOND RESURRECTION
ALL PEOPLE FROM ADAM TO THE END OF THE MILLENNIUM

The last and final resurrection of any kind for all eternity will be at this time. This is when all damned souls are raised to immortality at the end of the Millennial Reign. The wicked dead to be resurrected are all souls from Adam to the end of the thousand-year reign of Christ, excluding those who were sentenced 1,000 years earlier at the Judgment of the Nations (Mat. 25:31-46). This also includes those wicked who die during the Millennium. Yes, people can sin and die during the Millennial Reign.

> There shall be no more thence an infant of days, nor an old man that hath not filled his days: for the child shall die an hundred years old; but the sinner *being* an hundred years old shall be accursed (Isa. 65:20).

Just as there is a law of God in the New Testament (Rom. 2:14-15; 3:27; 4:3-5, 11-24; 7:16, 21, 23; 8:2, 23, 25; 9:31), there will always be laws in the future, even though grace abounds. All sin is the transgression of the law. Whoever sins breaks the law and obtains the death penalty (Ezek. 18:4; Rom. 6:23; 8:12-13). This is the way it has always been in any dispensation, under law or grace. When a person commits a death-penalty sin during the Millennium, he will be executed at any age, even if he is 100, even 1,000 years of age (Isa. 65:20).

The judgment during this time is more commonly recognized by the name, The Great White Throne Judgment. When people talk about judgment day, they are referring to this day. All who have part in this judgment will be sentenced to the lake of fire in a conscious, eternal and immortal existence. Immortality may seem like a fairy tale to some, but we will all be clothed in it at some point. All the damned will wish they were not immortal and they did just burn up to nothing, ceasing to exist. Honestly, I wish this were the case. I wish quite a few things in Scripture were not true. It would be wonderful to believe what so many deceived have tried to teach me about salvation.

Those good hearted folks believe once you are saved, you are always saved. They say being able to lose your salvation for any reason is not good news. But to a person who believes in Universalism, that all will be saved no matter what, telling them there is a hell is considered bad news. The gospel is horrifying news to most the world, so we can't have this as our standard for truth. Even the eternal security believers proclaim the existence of a hell that lost souls will be in forever. This is not positive, encouraging, or good news. We must be honest with Scripture, lay down all preconceived ideas, and conform our doctrinal beliefs to what is biblically taught.

Hell is real and there's a judgment for all, a judgment much closer than commonly thought (Mat. 10:28; Jn. 5:28-29; 12:24; Dan. 12:3; Acts 24:15; 1 Cor. 15:21, 34-50; Rev. 14:9-12; 20:4-6, 11-15). The reason for the Great White Throne Judgment is to give every man a just and legal proceeding before his eternal punishment (Acts 17:31; Ps. 9:8).

> But the LORD shall endure for ever: he hath prepared his throne for judgment. And he shall judge the world in righteousness, he shall minister judgment to the people in uprightness (Ps. 9:7-8).

> Because he hath appointed a day, in the which he will judge the world in righteousness by *that* man whom he hath ordained; *whereof* he hath given assurance unto all *men*, in that he hath raised him from the dead (Acts 17:31).

All the resurrected will be judged by the first fruit of all resurrections (1 Cor. 15:20, 23). This is the day of fulfillment for Philippians 2:10-11, when all knees in heaven, on earth, and under the earth shall bow with every tongue confessing that Jesus Christ is Lord.

At the time of this judgment, all wicked, unbelieving, and sinners will be judged and cast into the lake of fire by God (Mat. 10:28; Lk. 12:5). Yes, all unfaithful angels and demons as well. All ungodly, even if they are angelic DNA mixed with human DNA, whether giants of old (Gen. 6:1-4), or "alien" beings of today. They are all rebels against God and will be thrown into the lake of fire, which is where all the unjust and filthy will be confined forever.

Some angels are loose and free to continue in their rebellion, while others are bound. All await the same fate (1 Cor. 6:3; 1 Pt. 4; 2 Pt. 2:4; Jude 6-7; Rev. 12:7-12). No part of hell was created for man, and no man has to go there unless he continues to rebel against God's ways by following the devil (Jn. 3:16-20; 2 Pt. 3:9). For your sake, repent, follow the God who loves you, and have no part in the second resurrection.

> Then shall he say also unto them on the left hand, Depart from me, ye cursed, <u>into everlasting fire</u>, <u>prepared for the devil and his angels</u> (Mat. 25:41).

Some have said to me that they believe the resurrection of all men is at the same time. We have just proven otherwise, but to be fair, let's look at what the basis of their belief (John 5:29).

> Verily, verily, I say unto you, He that heareth my word, and believeth on him that sent me, hath everlasting life, and shall not come into condemnation; but is passed from death unto life. Verily, verily, I say unto you, The hour is coming, and now is, when the dead shall hear the voice of the Son of God: and they that hear shall live. For as the Father hath life in himself; so hath he given to the Son to have life in himself; And hath given him authority to execute judgment also, because he is the Son of man. Marvel not at this: for the

hour is coming, in the which all that are in the graves shall hear his voice, And shall come forth; they that have done good, unto the resurrection of life; and they that have done evil, unto the resurrection of damnation (John 5:24-29).

There is actually more than one resurrection, both with many phases. Revelation 20:4-15 is proof enough that there is more than one resurrection in time, since it calls the resurrection of the just, the first resurrection. That is then followed by at least one thousand years before the second resurrection, consisting of only the damned (Rev. 20:11-15). Daniel 12:2 is even used to prove the two resurrections happen at the same time.

And many of them that sleep in the dust of the earth shall awake, some to everlasting life, and some to shame *and* everlasting contempt (Dan. 12:2).

No time element is given, but Revelation 20 reveals detailed truth from this fact in Daniel. Teaching one resurrection is just as incorrect as teaching one future rapture. There are many of both to come. With that said, this concludes all the resurrections of the Bible, proving that John 5:24-29 is not referring to a certain day when all resurrections occur, rather just telling that all will be resurrected at some point in time.

To conclude the resurrection of the whole human race, I think it'll be fun to answer some questions everyone has had at some point. Eric Clapton had a hit called, "Tears in Heaven," inspired by the death of his four-year-old son. With all due respect to Mr. Clapton and the horror he lives through by the tragic death of his son, the first line of that song speaks volumes to the confusion people have concerning all aspects of the after-life. It is as follows:

> "Would you know my name
> If I saw you in heaven?"

This is a question all have about their loved ones in heaven. Of course no one says that about their loved ones in hell. The cruel truth is more people die and go to hell than those who enter heaven. Countless Christian funerals have been given to lost souls. This has been for the benefit of the living, but in the end gives everyone a false sense of security with a warm embrace of misunderstanding to salvation truth. It would be wise to let go of the hand of offense now, learn God's ways, and live.

> Open rebuke *is* better than secret love. Faithful *are* the wounds of a friend; but the kisses of an enemy *are* deceitful (Prov. 27:5-6).

So, If Eric Clapton is a follower of Christ at the time of his death, or at the time of the rapture, then yes, he will know his son's name. Not only that, but Eric Clapton will remember who he is, possess all his memories, and still look the same, but without any physical defects or aged appearance. Everyone will have their own body, not some new body or the appearance of another. It is the body that is resurrected, not a new one given. Damaged, scarred, and wrinkled grains reproduce perfect bodies in normal reproduction. There is no deviation in visual aspect of original and reproduced grain. All grains reproduce their own size, shape, and individual characteristics.

You will still be you, just a better you that is immortal and incorruptible. A you that will never be tempted by the devil or your flesh. All relationships you had on earth will remain in heaven as far as friendship and love. Of course, there is no marriage or sex, because we won't need to keep our race alive, because we will be immortal. All will have their own color, gender, physical attributes, size, shape, features, characteristics, and be precisely the same. Size will vary only if one is malnourished or obese on earth, but natural body structure remains. Resurrected bodies will be like Christ only in the sense of immortality (Jn. 12:24; 1 Cor. 15:36-54; Phil. 3:21).

THE RESURRECTION OF THE GIANTS

This is an extra piece for the sake of being thorough and bringing in an aspect never taught in church. We briefly brushed over giants a few pages back, so I want to expound on it since the giants are part human. They were an ungodly half-breed of angelic being mixed with human being. This is something like one of today's half breeds called a liger, which is half tiger, and half lion. The angels and humans are able to do this because they are alike in many ways. Both are called "sons of God" depending on certain conditions.

Angels are sons of God by creation (Gen. 6:4; Job 1:6; 2:1; 38:4-7), which is the same with Adam (Lk. 3:38). Both have been given the same appearance for the most part. Angels who sinned by marrying women did so by giving up their first estate (2 Pt. 2:4; Jude 6-7), that is, they gave up their immortal body, which is what the righteous long for. The point is, this angelic half-breed is damned with no chance of a resurrection.

> There were giants in the earth in those days; and also after that, when the sons of God came in unto the daughters of men, and they bare *children* to them, the same *became* mighty men which *were* of old, men of renown (Gen. 6:4).

There were giants in two periods of time according to Genesis 6:4, before the flood and after the flood. The purpose of this first explosion of fallen angels who lived with the daughters of men was to corrupt the human race and do away with pure stock of the human DNA line so that Jesus, the seed of the woman, could not come into the world. This plan would have successfully fended off Satan's doom, along with all the angels who rebelled against God with him (Gen. 3:15; Isa. 14:12-14; Ezek. 28:11-17; Rev. 12:1-12). I'm not going to spend much time proving that there were giant human beings, but I am aware of the refutes.

The fact is that there were many giants in Scripture and this can be plainly seen. A "valley of the giants" is mentioned in Joshua 15:8; 18:16, which is the valley of Rephaim, the name of one of the divisions of giant races (Gen. 14:5; 15:20; 2 Sam. 5:18, 22; 23:13; 1 Chr. 11:15; 14:9; Isa. 17:5). The Rephaims were well-known giants in ancient times, but regrettably, the King James writers in the early 1600's wrongfully translated their name for "dead" (Job 26:5; Ps. 88:10; Prov. 2:18; 9:18; 21:16; Isa.14:8; 26:19) and "deceased" (Isa. 26:14).

> *They are* dead, they shall not live; *they are* deceased (Rephaim), they shall not rise: therefore hast thou visited and destroyed them, and made all their memory to perish (Isa. 26:14).

The giant races have no resurrection. Rephaim is translated "giant" in Deuteronomy 2:11, 20; 3:11, 13; Joshua 12:4; 13:12; 15:8; 18:16; 2 Samuel 21:16, 18, 20, 22; 1

Chronicles 20:4, 6, 8. Many nations of giants existed and are listed as Kenites, Kenizzites, Kadmonites, Hittites, Perizzites, Rephaims, Amorites, Canaanites, Girgashites, Jebusites, Hivites, Anakims, Emims, Horims, Avims, Zamzummims, Caphtorims, and Nephilims (Gen. 6:4; 14:5-6; 15:19-21; Ex. 3:8, 17; 23:23; Dt. 2:10-12, 20-23; 3:11-13; 7:1; 20:17; Josh. 12:4-8; 13:3; 15:8; 17:15; 18:16).

> O LORD our God, *other* lords beside thee have had dominion over us: *but* by thee only will we make mention of thy name (Isa. 26:13).

The Rephaim were the other lords of Isaiah 26:13. Giant nations had dominion over the land of Israel for much time. Many giant nations mentioned above claimed the promised land as their own. I'm sure they had direction from their fallen angelic fathers.

> They shall not rise because God visited and destroyed them (Isa. 26:14).

This clearly teaches that the giants, or Rephaim, have no resurrection like Isaiah and the dead of Israel do, as referred to in Isaiah 26:19.

> Thy dead *men* shall live, *together with* my dead body shall they arise. Awake and sing, ye that dwell in dust: for thy dew *is as* the dew of herbs, and the earth shall cast out the dead (Isa. 26:19).

Giants have angelic DNA because they were the offspring of fallen angels, not pure-bred men who do have a resurrection. Recent biblical researchers and watchers have posed that the giants may rise in the last days and be the supernatural army in Joel 2:1-11. I believe that supernatural army consist of all glorified saints taking back the earth at the Second Coming (Zech. 14:5; Jude 14-15; Rev. 19:11-16). Others believe the giants will rise during the Tribulation. They base it on Jesus' words in Matthew 24:37 when He says as the days of Noah *were,* so shall also the coming of the Son of man be. What was going on in Noah's day that was different than our own that may stand out? "There were giants in the earth in those days ..." (Gen. 6:4). I believe there is truth in that theory, but I'll save that detail for the last three books in this series.

Some believe the demons of today are actually the disembodied spirit of the dead giants. They get this theory from the Book of Enoch. Some theologians believe demons are the spirits of the pre-Adamites, an age of human beings that existed before the flood of Genesis 1:2, called the flood of Lucifer. This has its origin in the Gap Theory. No matter what your belief, we now know that the giants of old do not have part in a resurrection, and neither do demons, though all will be classed together with the wicked in the lake of fire at the conclusion of the second resurrection. We can't question the fairness of this, we can only believe that God is fair and just.

Chapter 6

UNVEILING RAPTURES THROUGH TIME

REDEEMED MAN SOUL AND SPIRIT ONLY

I'll remind you that the word rapture, literally means "the act of transporting." In terms of the rapture of the church, my church family that watches end-time teaching programs have become familiar with terms such as: "caught up" (1 Thess. 4:17; 2 Cor. 12:4); "receive you unto myself" (Jn. 14:1-3); and "come up hither" (Rev. 4:1; 11:12). We know that Jesus is coming down from heaven to the earth's sky to <u>call the righteous up</u>. We know He is right out of the earth's atmosphere when He receives the redeemed unto Himself. We understand that the church will be <u>caught up</u>, and some understand that the 144,000 will be told to <u>come up</u> hither, which is the same wording used for John in Revelation 4:1. My point is that everyone thinks there has to be a calling upward in the sky to correctly be a rapture. The truth is that a rapture is simply the act of transporting from one place to another.

This word "rapture" has become demonized by many who profess to be Christian, and among those who do not believe, they simply mock. I've experienced a great deal of mockers for how outspoken I am about this doctrine, but this is no surprise, it isn't even new or clever. Let's show just how silly it is for the mockers to scoff at the word "rapture."

> Knowing this first, that there shall come in the last days scoffers, walking after their own lusts, And saying, Where is the promise of his coming? for since the fathers fell asleep, all things continue as *they were* from the beginning of the creation (2 Pet. 3:3-4).

In Matthew 13:19, the words "catcheth away" is used for what the devil does when he takes (transports from one place to another) the Word of the kingdom from those who hear, but don't understand. The words "catcheth away" are translated from the Greek word "harpazo," which again is the same word we derive our term "rapture" (1 Thess. 4:17). Just notice the simplicity of what you've seen. Catching away means the same as catching up. The direction in which something or someone is taken bears no relevance for it to soundly be called a rapture. A rapture is simply transporting from one place to another.

Let's see a few more biblical uses that are used for the Greek word, "harpazo" (GSN-<G726>). Matthew 11:12; John 6:15; and Acts 23:10 all use it with the translation being, "take by force." These references have nothing to do with the rapture, though a transporting from one place to another was happening, or at least trying to take place as seen in John 6:15. Then, in John 10:12, the word "catch" is used in showing the wolf catching a sheep. A few verses later harpazo is used again, but this time translated "pluck" (Jn. 10:28-29).

True as it is that John 10:25-29 is a pillar for the unconditional eternal security believers, isn't it possible for the devil to pluck, catch, catch away, or pull the unrighteous to hell at death since he has legal authority over their souls (Jn. 8:31-34; Rom. 6:1-23; 1 Jn. 3:8-10)? Another use of the word has been translated, "catch away or up" (Acts 8:39; 2 Cor. 12:2-

4; 1 Thess. 4:17; Rev. 12:5). "Pull" in Jude 23 tells Christians to save the willing with fear, <u>pulling</u> them out of the fate of eternal hell. "Pulling" was translated from the Greek word "harpazo." We pull our money out of the bank every time we go to an ATM. We just simply transport it from one place to another. My intention here is to show you the simplicity of the word "rapture," so it won't appear so taboo.

Well, there have been many raptures through time. In keeping with the outline in chapter 4, we'll go right down that outline without even blinking. Since you've made it through the resurrection outline, this will be a snap. All the redeemed souls of the dead were transported from earth at the time of their death. Where they were raptured to has been the subject of debate among mankind for millenniums. But I'm convinced that those reading even this far into this book really do believe all scripture is authoritative, inerrant, and infallible (2 Pt. 1:20-21; 2 Tim. 2:15; 3:16-17). I have faith that you will believe the Word of God. It is referenced for you to examine at any time (Acts 17:11; 2 Tim. 2:15).

Soul and Spirit Only
All Righteous Who Died Before Jesus Rose and Went to Abraham's Bosom
All Righteous from Abraham's Bosom to Heaven
All Righteous Who Have Died After Jesus Rose and Went to Heaven

At this time only, we will be referring to the righteous souls and spirits of a people who have died. There is no resurrection in any of these next few examples. All the dead immediately go (transported) to one of two places: heaven or hell. But before the resurrection of Jesus, the righteous went to a chamber in hell called, Abraham's Bosom (Lk. 16:22), or paradise (Lk. 23:43), which is located inside the earth (Mat. 12:40; Eph. 4:8-10).

They were apparently transported there by angels, unless Lazarus was an isolated incident (Lk. 16:22). When Jesus rose from the dead, He transported all the righteous captives in hell from Abraham's Bosom to the earth (Mat. 27:52-53), and then to heaven (Ps. 68:18; Eph. 4:8), which is now where all saints go when they die (2 Cor. 5:8; Phil. 1:21-24; Heb. 1:23; Jas. 2:26; Rev. 6:9-11). Saints did not have direct access to heaven until Jesus defeated death, hell, and the grave, also taking away the sins of the righteous that were merely covered up until that point (Gal. 3:19; Heb. 7:17-23; 1 Tim. 2:5).

Soul and Spirit Only
Every Person in Heaven at His Coming for the Saints Before the Tribulation

1 Thessalonians 4:13-17 is one of the two most recognizable and famous rapture passages in the Bible, but there is a seldom known truth hidden in plain sight. This passage gives us the fact that Jesus will be bringing all human beings from heaven with Him to rapture the living in Christ at that moment. Bringing the saints of heaven to earth is a transporting from one place to another. This is a massive rapture of many souls taking place moments before their physical resurrection and rapture back to heaven. The truth of this begins a few verses before this passage.

> To the end he may stablish your hearts unblameable in holiness before God, even our Father, <u>at the coming of our Lord Jesus Christ with all his saints</u> (1 Thess. 3:13).

The saints here are not the ones already resurrected that rose when He did (Mat. 27:52-53), nor are they the two anointed ones standing by the Lord of the whole earth (Zech. 4:14). The two witnesses will not return to earth until at least 3 ½ years later to begin their 1,260-day mission (Rev. 11:3-12). They will be resurrected and raptured seven years after the rapture of the church. 1 Thessalonians 4:16-17 is the famously known rapture passage that is mostly read by itself, while overlooking all truths conveyed by the Holy Spirit.

> But I would not have you to be ignorant, brethren, concerning them which are asleep, that ye sorrow not, even as others which have no hope. For if we believe that Jesus died and rose again, <u>even so them also which sleep in Jesus will God bring with him</u> (1 Thess. 4:13-14).

I used to always picture Jesus coming back to the air to call us up, and I never pictured Him with a multitude of people. I always pictured Him alone, but He will be coming back with the saints in heaven. I've seen videos online paired with hour long teachings showing Jesus flying through space from the constellation Orion. Simple truths are often unseen or exchanged for extravagant imaginations and human reasoning. I guess this image comes because we focus mostly on 1 Thessalonians 4:16-17 to teach the rapture, overlooking the rest of the entire Book. 1 Thessalonians teaches the rapture and coming of Christ in every chapter (1 Thess. 1:10; 2:12, 19; 3:13; 4:13-18; 5:1-11, 23). Jesus will not be coming alone when He raptures the church. He will not be travelling at the speed of light through space. There will be a door, literally a portal from heaven to the sky of earth (Rev. 4:1; 19:11).

1 Thessalonians 3:13 refers to the rapture when Christ meets the saints and church in the air (1 Thess. 4:16-17) and

takes them to heaven where they are presented before God the Father and established in eternal and unblameable holiness by God. This is sufficient proof that unforfeitable life is given for the first time at the resurrection. Salvation is always called a hope for the believer, because it can be lost if you die in disobedience to the covenant (Mat. 7:13-14; 18:8-9; 19:28-29; Mk. 10:29-30; Lk. 18:29-30; Rom. 2:7; 6:21-23; Gal. 6:7-8; 1 Tim. 1:16; 4:8; 6:12, 19; Tit. 1:2; 3:7; 1 Pet. 1:5, 9, 13, 3:7; 1 Jn. 2:25; Jude 1:20-24; Dan. 12:2). Sin always brings the spiritual death penalty.

We must remain holy. The death of Jesus Christ is the assurance of salvation for all who will believe (Mat. 26:28; Rom. 5:6-11; 1 Pet. 2:24), but belief implies obedience free from sin (Jn. 3:36; Rom. 6:1-23; 8:1-13; Gal. 5:16-25; Heb. 5:9; Jas. 1:22-25; 2:14-26; 5:19-20; etc.). The resurrection of Jesus Christ is the assurance of resurrection for all men (1 Thess. 5:10; Jn. 14:19; Rom. 5:10; 6:5-8; 1 Cor. 15:4-23; 2 Tim. 2:11).

There is a rapture verse that surrounds itself with the teaching that one must remain holy and pure after Jesus has made us that way. In fact, all rapture verses are surrounded in such a manner. The rapture is motivation for holy living right now.

> Beloved, now are we the sons of God, and it doth not yet appear what we shall be: but we know that, when he shall appear, we shall be like him; for we shall see him as he is. And every man that hath this hope in him purifieth himself, even as he is pure (1 Jn. 3:2-3).

This is a rapture of all who die in Christ. He will bring them back from heaven to be given resurrected bodies (1 Thess. 4:14; Jn. 5:28-29; 1 Cor. 15:20-23, 35-58; Phil. 3:21).

The dead in Christ will rise before the living are changed (1 Thess. 4:16; 1 Cor. 15:23, 51-58; Phil. 3:21; Jn. 5:28-29). But this is as far as we will venture here. Even a transporting from heaven to earth in a spirit body is classified as a rapture. Even Christians at death who were raptured to heaven in their spirit body look forward to the resurrection of their sleeping bodies (2 Cor. 5:8; Phil. 1:21-24; Heb. 12:22-23; Rev. 6:9-11), which is preceded by another transportation by God from one place to another. There really is nothing hard to believe when it comes to the rapture as long as we can get over the word not being found in the Bible, because the teaching is everywhere, and written long before 1830.

RAPTURES REDEEMED MAN NATURAL BODY

I appreciate you taking the time to learn and understand the non-traditional raptures that happen countless times per day. Now, without further ado, I present to you the raptures of the saints in times past. In case this is new to you, there is a list of righteous men from biblical record that have been transported (raptured) from earth to heaven, and in one instance, from one city on earth to another city on earth. We have spoken of Enoch and Elijah, but the list goes beyond them. The common list includes: Enoch, Moses, Elijah, Isaiah, Philip, Paul, John. Spoiler alert! Two of these men were not raptured, and there are two more groups of people that have not been mentioned. Have a hint and a reminder: we are currently only speaking about righteous, natural men.

NATURAL BODY
ENOCH AND ELIJAH

Enoch and Elijah were spoken about in the resurrection section, so we'll keep this brief, saving the proof of their identity as the two witnesses for the section on the rapture of those two great witnesses for Christ (Rev. 11:3-12). These two men were raptured to heaven before anyone. They were not resurrected, nor were they changed from mortality into immortality. They reside before God the Father and God the Son in their natural bodies until they are sent back to earth to stand against the Antichrist, the false prophet, and the enemies of Israel. They will turn the hearts of Israel back to God in the wilderness (Rev. 12:13-17), just like Moses and Joshua did in the days after Egyptian bondage. They will both be killed at least four days before the Second Coming (Rev. 11:7, 11-12).

What's really interesting is that they were both taken to heaven, not Abraham's Bosom (Gen. 5:24; 2 Ki. 2:11; Zech. 4:14; Mal. 4:5-6; Heb. 11:5; Lk. 16:22). Jesus had not even died on the cross, so how were they able to go to heaven before then, ahead of all saints before them? I believe the answer is that they had not died, so Satan had no legal claim on them to keep them captive (Eph. 4:8-11; Heb. 2:14-15). Even the sinful devil could go to the throne to present Himself before God, so why not natural man (Job 1:6 – 2:7; Rev. 12:10)?

These two men will be translated two more times at least. First, they have to be translated from heaven to earth to be Christ's witnesses for 1,260 days. Can you imagine living in heaven for thousands of years, but then have to come back wearing sackcloth for 3.5 years during the most dreadful era in existence? Enoch has been in heaven for over 5,000 years, while Elijah has been with him for more than 3,000 years, totaling more than 8,000 earth years.

After their earth mission, they will be raptured after their resurrection as they ascend in a cloud in front of all their enemies (Rev. 11:12). They will join the rest of the glorified saints in heaven at just the right time. All will have part in the Marriage Supper of the Lamb before coming back to earth to take it back from all unjust and wicked governments and man (Rev. 19:1-16; Joel 2:1-11).

There is one more piece to Elijah's story as far as recorded in Scripture. He was actually raptured (transported from one place to another) one more time in history, making another trip to earth and back. This is another non-traditional rapture, but a rapture by definition nonetheless. We have to be comfortable with the rapture of the church, for many raptures have already occurred in several different fashions. Many more are to come. So, remember the transfiguration on top of the mountain (Mat. 17:1-12)? This is an event when Jesus took three of His disciples to the top of a mountain. This was most likely for a time of refreshment, fasting, and prayer as Jesus often did.

During their time on the mountain, referred to as The Mount of Transfiguration, Moses and Elijah appeared to them (Jesus, Peter, James, and John his brother) (Mat. 17:1). The reason for the appearance to Jesus is not fully stated, but there was undoubtedly a revelation and confirmation of many things given to Jesus to assure Him of His earthly ministry and embolden Him for the things He must suffer. After all, Christ just foretold His death in the previous verses (Mat. 16:21-23), then admonished all who follow Him to get ready to bear their cross as well (Mat. 16:24-28). The verses before the transfiguration are more important than all the rapture study in the world. Please meditate on what they mean before moving forward.

> Then said Jesus unto his disciples, If any *man* will come after me, let him deny himself, and take up his cross, and follow me. For whosoever will save his life shall lose it: and whosoever will lose his life for my sake shall find it. For what is a man profited, if he shall gain the whole world, and lose his own soul? or what shall a man give in exchange for his soul? For the Son of man shall come in the glory of his Father with his angels; and then he shall reward every man according to his works (Mat. 16:24-27).

As for the appearance of Elijah, he still had never died and had been living in heaven in his natural body for just about one thousand years at the time (2 Ki. 2; Mal. 4:5-6; Zech. 4:11-14; Rev. 11:3-11). He has now been there around three thousand years, as he is one of the two anointed ones that stand by the Lord of the whole earth (Zech. 4:14). So he had to be transported from heaven in order to confirm many things to Jesus.

What a life Elijah has had. You know, you can experience such a glorious future as well. You and I can even be very close friends with Elijah as long as we take the commands of Jesus seriously. We must accept Jesus as a fact that is believed, and followed, or your mental acceptance of a fact would become dead, vain, and worthless (Jas. 2:14-26). We must follow Jesus daily, not just on Sunday or when it is acceptable to man, but habitually to the point of death. Deny all self-interests and self-pursuits that are contrary to God's ways. If sin is continued and you die in sin, then you'll have part in the second resurrection instead of having part in the glorious future God has for you

(Mk. 8:34; Lk. 9:23; Jn. 10:26-28; 12:26; 17:17; Rom. 6:16-23; 8:12-13; Gal. 5:19-24; 6:7-8; Col. 1:23; 2:6-7; 3:1-10).

And Jesus said unto him, No man, having put his hand to the plough, and looking back, is fit for the kingdom of God (Lk. 9:62).

NATURAL BODY
MOSES

Moses is a great man of God. I in no way would belittle him, and if he was raptured to heaven at 120 years of age instead of simply dying, then I would assuredly report that here today. Claims of his rapture just cannot be validated with Scripture no matter how many people want to plead and argue that he was taken to heaven without experiencing death. The only rapture Moses has been a part of since his death has been at the Mount of Transfiguration with Elijah, and when Jesus set the captives free from Abraham's bosom after His resurrection. Was Moses one of the resurrected Old Testament saints who bodily rose and appeared unto many (Mat. 27:52-53), or was he one of the souls and spirits of just men whose bodies were not resurrected (Eph. 4:8-10; Heb. 12:23)? I wouldn't dare speculate, nor does it matter. He was one of them and he was assuredly transported from paradise in the earth to heaven some two thousand years ago.

As for the transfiguration, it occurred while Moses was still being held captive in one of hell's chambers that was set aside at that time for the safe dwelling of the saints (Lk. 16:19-31; Eph. 4:8-19; Heb. 2:14-15). Moses had been dead for more than fifteen hundred years and his body was then in corruption (Dt. 34; Jude 9). He was evidently brought up from paradise beneath the earth in his spirit body, proving the eternal existence in a state of full consciousness after death (Lk. 16:19-31; Ps. 16:1; Heb. 12:23). The righteous dead even wear clothes and the lost in hell even thirst (Lk. 16:24; Rev. 6:9-11), proving that the soul of Moses wasn't ghost-like in appearance. Jesus, Peter, James, and John saw Moses as a tangible person just as easily as they saw Elijah in a physical appearance. Remember that Jesus had not become the first fruits of the resurrection yet (1 Cor. 15:20, 23), so Moses was not in a resurrected body either.

Many people identify Moses as one of the two witnesses (Rev. 11:7-12). They believe he was raptured like Enoch and Elijah, but if he were taken to heaven without seeing death, then Scriptures are deceitful concerning his death. God had even prepared him for death when He told Moses to go up into Mount Abarim, behold the land of Canaan, and die on the mount (Num. 27:12-14; Dt. 32:50; 34:5-8). He was not permitted to go into the promised land because of his sin of striking the rock instead of speaking to it (Num. 20:10-15).

But if someone were to play devil's advocate and say God raised Moses from the dead so he could be one of the two witnesses, then I would remind that person that it is appointed for man to die once (Heb. 9:27), so if Moses had been raised from his natural death in his natural body, then he would have two appointments for death, which is contrary to the teaching of Paul in Hebrews 9. Moses was appointed for that death on the mountain. Also, if God was going to raise him from the dead, then why wait until he was buried? Moses is often thought to have been raptured, but this could not be further from the plain statements of Scripture.

> And he buried him in a valley in the land of Moab, over against Bethpeor: but no man knoweth of his sepulchre unto

this day. And Moses *was* an hundred and twenty years old when he died... (Dt. 34:6-7).

Moses is also thought of to be one the two witnesses because it would seem that one of the two witnesses have power over the rain, like Elijah, and the other has power over plaques, like Moses had. If the truth be known, the two witnesses receive the same power, and if power given by God were the standard for who holds the identity of the two witnesses, then Elisha should be one of them, for he had a double portion of Elijah's spirit and power. The only true rapture Moses had in his life time was a typifying of the rapture, not an actual physical transportation himself (Jude 9; Dt. 34:5-8).

Exodus 19 shows Moses ascending up the mountain and God descending with a voice of the trumpet that was exceedingly loud. The ascending of a righteous people with the descending of God to meet the righteous certainly is in harmony with the rapture of the church, especially with the voice of a trumpet (Ex.19:16; 1 Cor. 15:51-54; 1 Thess. 4:16-17; Rev.4:1). Moses has been transported from one place to another on several occasions, but a physical rapture did not take place for him in his earthly life. Myth busted!

NATURAL BODY
ISAIAH

This is an interesting one for me. Isaiah was a prophet who wrote an amazing book modeled like a miniature Bible at a time in history that was well before the collaboration of the Bible. There hadn't even been a single word formed in the New Testament yet. The book of Isaiah has 66 chapters corresponding with the 66 books of the Bible. 39 chapters were written in the first section that dealt with law and judgment. This corresponded with the message of the 39 books of the Old Testament. 27 chapters were written in the second section, and this corresponded with the 27 books of the New Testament both in number and message of comfort and redemption through Jesus, the Messiah.

The purpose of Isaiah's messages was to make God's message clear to Israel that judgment would be inevitable for persisting in sin. God wanted to also unveil the eternal and final plans He has for them in the perfect restoration coming under their Messiah (Isa. 9:6-7; 11:10-12; 66:22-24). This prophet thoroughly wrote about the past, present, and future all the way into the Millennial Reign.

One of the most famous of Isaiah's prophecies was that of the suffering Messiah. Isaiah 53 accurately predicts and describes the time of Jesus' arrest and crucifixion. Isaiah 53 is even foreign to many Jews, because it's truth points exclusively to the New Testament Jesus as their Messiah, the one who they have rejected (Rom. 11:17-25).

Isaiah 6 is also a well-known passage. I was unfamiliar with it in my late 20's when the leader of the dance and drama team at my church asked me to play the angel of Isaiah 6:1-8. I had long hair and a muscular build in those days. I was a long term believer, but it wasn't until the age of 26 that I became a true follower. I was so hungry for God and Bible truth that I dove in and have never come up for air. I found that I needed God more than a heartbeat. The well-known passage is below, and this is where many get the idea that Isaiah was taken to heaven like Paul and John (2 Cor. 12:1-7; Rev. 4:1).

> In the year that king Uzziah died I saw also the Lord sitting upon a throne, high and lifted up, and his train filled the temple. Above it stood the seraphims: each one had six wings; with twain he covered his face, and with twain he covered his

feet, and with twain he did fly. And one cried unto another, and said, Holy, holy, holy, *is* the LORD of hosts: the whole earth *is* full of his glory. And the posts of the door moved at the voice of him that cried, and the house was filled with smoke. Then said I, Woe *is* me! for I am undone; because I *am* a man of unclean lips, and I dwell in the midst of a people of unclean lips: for mine eyes have seen the King, the LORD of hosts. Then flew one of the seraphims unto me, having a live coal in his hand, *which* he had taken with the tongs from off the altar: And he laid *it* upon my mouth, and said, Lo, this hath touched thy lips; and thine iniquity is taken away, and thy sin purged. Also I heard the voice of the Lord, saying, Whom shall I send, and who will go for us? Then said I, Here *am* I; send me (Isa. 6:1-8).

As you can see, it's very easily mistaken as a rapture of Isaiah. It's also easily understood to see why this passage is so beloved. It strikes at the heart of man who longs to see God in all His splendor. I fell in love with this passage the first time I heard it, as do so many loving souls. Truth be told, I had always thought Isaiah was translated in an atom of time in order for him to fall before the throne of the Most High God in His temple, so I have no ill thoughts about the intelligence of those who hold to this belief. I'd like to give another mode of thought at the event from Isaiah 6. This is what I believe after studying this event further since the first time I have heard it. If indeed you believe Isaiah was translated, see if you don't change the scope of your thinking on this natural body rapture.

The temple God appeared to Isaiah in was not the heavenly temple, which does exist (Ex. 25:1-9, 40; Heb. 8:5), but rather the temple that stood in Isaiah's day. The Bible does not state the exact temple he was in, but it must have been Solomon's temple, since that is the temple in use in the prophet's day. The Bible also does not state that Isaiah was in heaven, as is clear from John's experience in Revelation 4:1 – Revelation 5:14. However, Isaiah 6 does mention the earth.

> And one cried unto another, and said, Holy, holy, holy, *is* the LORD of hosts: <u>the whole earth</u> *is* full of his glory (Isa. 6:3).

Isaiah 6:9-12 references the people of the earth, so the indication is that the experience was a vision on earth while Isaiah was in the temple. Could God not appear to be on His throne with His robe filling the temple? Could a vision not include fiery angels called seraphims who cry, "Holy, holy, holy...? Those words have come from these angels' lips from their beginning, and is what they will always do.

> Holy, holy, holy, Lord God Almighty, which was, and is, and is to come (Rev. 4:8).

Some would say Isaiah must have been taken to heaven because a natural man cannot see God face to face and live. "...for mine eyes have seen the King, the LORD of hosts" (vs. 5). There was an old superstition that if one saw God he would die. This is still the dominating belief accepted as fact from most churched people. The basis of this belief is most likely founded in Exodus 33:20. Because of this, some have concluded that this is proof that Isaiah went to heaven where he would not die by seeing the Lord.

> And he said, Thou canst not see my face: for there shall no man see me, and live (Ex. 33:20).

One problem with that understanding is that it is not an absolute that men die when seeing the Lord. As far as seeing God face to face on earth without dying, we have at least forty appearances from God to man without the result of death. Jacob made the statement that his life was preserved because he also was under the impression that man would die if he saw God's face.

> And Jacob called the name of the place Peniel: for I have seen God face to face, and my life is preserved (Gen.32:30).

Gideon feared the same outcome by seeing the Lord's face, or else language means nothing. God assured Gideon that he would not die.

> And when Gideon perceived that he *was* an angel of the LORD, Gideon said, Alas, O Lord GOD! for because I have seen an angel of the LORD face to face. And the LORD said unto him, Peace *be* unto thee; fear not: thou shalt not die (Judges 6:22-23).

One more proof of this superstitious belief is from Manoah, that seeing God would bring death.

> And Manoah said unto his wife, We shall surely die, because we have seen God (Judges 13:22).

Before explaining what really took place for Isaiah in chapter 6 of his book, lets conclude the proof that God can be seen without harm to man. It is good for us to learn Bible facts along our journey so what we hear cannot be snatched away from us (Mat. 13:19). Many men have seen God with their own eyes: (Gen. 18:2, 33; 32:24-30; Ex. 24:10; 33:11; Josh. 5:13; Isa. 6; Ezek. 1:26-28; Dan. 7:9-14; 10:5-6; Acts 7:56-59; Rev. 4:2-5; 5:1-7).

> And ye said, Behold, the LORD our God hath shewed us his glory and his greatness, and we have heard his voice out of the midst of the fire: we have seen this day that God doth talk with man, and <u>he liveth</u> (Dt. 5:24).

Many believe wrongly about verses like Exodus 33:20, John 1:18, and 1 John 4:12.

> And he said, Thou canst not see my face: for there shall no man see me, and live (Ex. 33:20).

The truth is that man cannot see God's face <u>in His full glory and in the light that He dwells in</u>, which is what no mortal man has seen, nor can see. God exists and remains in limitless and dateless glory which no man has ever seen nor can see, but has been seen out of His glory on numerous occasions by natural man as proved from the following verses.

> And it shall come to pass, while my glory passeth by, that I will put thee in a clift of the rock, and will cover thee with my hand while I pass by: And I will take away mine hand, and thou shalt see my back parts: but my face shall not be seen (Ex. 33:22-23).

> Who only hath immortality, dwelling in the light which no man can approach unto; whom no man hath seen, nor can see: to whom *be* honour and power everlasting. Amen (1 Tim. 6:16).

More proof of natural men being face to face or in the sight of God: (Gen. 3:8-19; 5:22-24; 6:8-9; 12:7; 17:1-22; 18:1-2, 22; 19:1; 26:2-4, 24; 28:12-15; 32:24-32; 35:1, 9-15; Ex. 19:11-24; 24:1-18; 33:9-11; 34:5-7; Lev. 9:23-24; Num. 12:4-5; 14:10-12, 14; 16:19-30, 41-50; 20:6-13; 22:20, 23-27, 31-38; 23:3-10, 16-24; Dt. 5:4, 22-29; 31:2, 15-16; Judg.

2:1-5; Josh. 5:13-15; 1 Sam. 3:10, 21; 1 Ki. 19:11-18; 1 Chr. 21:16-17; 2 Chr. 3:1; Job 42:5; Ezek. 1:2-28; 8:1-4; 9:1-4; 10:1-5, 7-22; 40:1-4, 6, 8-9, 11-19, 24, 28, 32, 35, 45-48; 41:1, 4-5, 13, 15; 42:1, 13, 15-20; 43:1-7; Dan. 7:9-14; 10:5-9; Amos 9:1; Zech. 1:8-20; 2:1-13; 3:1-2; 4:1-5; 5:2-5, 10; 6:4-5; Acts 7:54-60; Heb. 11:5-7; Jude 1:14-15; Rev. 1:10-18; 4:2-11; 5:1-13; 6:16; 7:9-17; 8:3-5; 11:16; 12:5; 14:1-5; 19:1-10; 21:3-7; 22:1-5, 8-9).

NATURAL BODY
PHILIP

And he commanded the chariot to stand still: and they went down both into the water, both Philip and the eunuch; and he baptized him. And when they were come up out of the water, <u>the Spirit of the Lord caught away Philip</u>, that the eunuch <u>saw him no more</u>: and he went on his way rejoicing. <u>But Philip was found at Azotus</u>: and passing through he preached in all the cities, till he came to <u>Caesarea</u> (Acts 8:38-40).

There's not much of anything said in Scripture concerning this great man of faith, but there is enough to paint a picture of who he was and even where he lived. His story begins in Acts 6.

And in those days, when the number of the disciples was multiplied, there arose a murmuring of the Grecians against the Hebrews, because their widows were neglected in the daily ministration. Then the twelve called the multitude of the disciples unto them, and said, It is not reason that we should leave the word of God, and serve tables. Wherefore, brethren, look ye out among you seven men of honest report, full of the Holy Ghost and wisdom, whom we may appoint over this business (Acts 6:1-3).

The church chose seven men and the apostles laid hands on them and prayed, setting them apart for the business of taking care of the widows (Acts 6:3, 5-6). The seven men were Stephen, a man full of faith and of the Holy Ghost, and Philip, Prochorus, Nicanor, Timon, Parmenas, and Nicolas a proselyte of Antioch (Acts 6:5). One of the apostles that laid hands on these seven men was a man named Philip (Jn. 1:43). He was chosen by Jesus in Galilee to be one of the twelve disciples and apostles in Jesus' earthly ministry, but is not the Philip that got raptured in his natural body, who is one of the seven (Acts 6:1-6). The Apostle Philip's introduction in Scripture begins so beautifully I simply can't forsake spelling it out. What a proclamation of pure, unwavering faith!

> The day following Jesus would go forth into Galilee, and findeth Philip, and saith unto him, Follow me. Now Philip was of Bethsaida, the city of Andrew and Peter. Philip findeth Nathanael, and saith unto him, We have found him, of whom Moses in the law, and the prophets, did write, Jesus of Nazareth, the son of Joseph (John 1:43-45).

Philip the Evangelist is the one who was caught away by the Holy Spirit and must be carefully distinguished from Philip the Apostle (one of the twelve disciples). We know very little about these seven men apart from Stephen (Acts 6:5 – Acts 8:2; 22:20) and Philip (Act 6:5; 8:1-40; 21:8). Though there is little told pertaining to him, the little we have is significant. As stated, he is first introduced to us as one of the seven selected by the early church in Jerusalem to take charge of the daily assistance of benevolence to the poor widows (Acts 6). And when this work is hindered by the outbreak of persecution following on the death of Stephen, we find him at once departing to enter active missionary work elsewhere (Acts 8).

While in Samaria, the angel of the Lord spoke unto Philip, saying, "Arise, and go toward the south unto the way that goeth down from Jerusalem unto Gaza, which is desert" (Acts 8:26). Philip was obedient to leave a rattling revival and a city with all its amenities to go to the desert to preach to one soul. Philip was not even told why he was to go south or even how far. Gaza was 100 miles from the revival, but he immediately began this journey that resulted in the salvation of a man of Ethiopia, a eunuch of great authority under Candace, queen of the Ethiopians, who had the charge of all her treasure, and had come to Jerusalem to worship (Acts 8:27).

As they continued traveling together, they came across some water and the eunuch was then baptized. I can't say the story of Philip gets more exciting, because it's obvious this man was full of the Holy Spirit and was clearly hearing God's voice in acting as an ambassador for His kingdom, but the story does give a fact that is astounding.

> And when they were come up out of the water, the Spirit of the Lord caught away Philip, that the eunuch saw him no more: and he went on his way rejoicing (Acts 8:39).

A clear reference to a rapture: [caught away] Greek: *harpazo* (GSN-<G726>), to seize; catch away; pluck; pull or take away by force. The simple truth here is that Philip was raptured, as the Greek word used in Acts 8:39 is the same used in 1 Thessalonians 4:16-17. Philip's rapture is the only one in Scripture to be a transporting from one place to another in a physical body while remaining on earth.

My observation is just to show that there are many different kinds of raptures. Not all have to result in going to heaven, whether in a natural body to remain for thousands of years like Enoch (Gen. 5:22-24) and Elijah (2 Ki. 2), or just for a moment in time like Paul (2 Cor. 12:1-7) and John (Rev. 4-5). This kind of travel sure would save some ministries multi-millions of dollars in private jet costs. This is how the glorified saints will travel after the resurrection of the just.

One simple rule is that a biblical rapture is just an act of being transported from one place to another. Philip was taken about 25 miles away to Azotus by God the Holy Spirit in his physical, natural body, and for an intention God purposed. The proof of distance is seen by Scripture telling us he was taken to Caesarea (Acts 8:40), which is not Caesarea Philippi (Mat. 16:13), but a city built by Herod between Joppa and Mt. Carmel (Josephus, Antiquities, Book 16, 2:1). Philip settled here (Acts 21:8). Always when mentioned individually it refers to this city. Caesarea is about 60 miles south of Tyre and about this far from Jerusalem. The distance of travel is never a defining characteristic of a true rapture. It could be a mile away or as far as heaven is above this earth.

The soon rapture of the church is also set in time for a reason, which we will get further into in book 2 (mid-tribulation – chapter 5). All such raptures in Scripture are by God alone, and all with a divine purpose. The next time someone tells you there is no rapture, because it was only an invention of man from the 1830's, you can smile and gracefully disagree with absolute certainty.

NATURAL BODY
PAUL

It is not expedient for me doubtless to glory. I will come to visions and revelations of the Lord. I knew a man in Christ above fourteen years ago, (whether in the body, I cannot tell; or whether out of the body, I cannot tell: God knoweth;) <u>such an one caught up to the third heaven</u>. And I knew such a man, (whether in the body, or out of the body, I cannot tell: God knoweth;) How that he was caught up into paradise, and heard unspeakable words, which it is not lawful for a man to utter. Of such an one will I glory: yet of myself I will not glory, but in mine infirmities. For though I would desire to glory, I shall not be a fool; for I will say the truth: but *now* I forbear, lest any man should think of me above that which he seeth me *to be*, or *that* he heareth of me. And lest I should be exalted above measure through the abundance of the revelations, there was given to me a thorn in the flesh, the messenger of Satan to buffet me, lest I should be exalted above measure (2 Cor. 12:1-7).

Verse 1 tells us that Paul was speaking about a revelation he received. A revelation is an unveiling of things not known before and which God alone could make known. This is also why John was taken to heaven (Rev. 1:1-2). In verse 2, Paul reveals that he was unsure if he was in the third heaven in his natural body or if it were a vision.

The Annotated Dake Bible says, "God often used vision or mental pictures to impart revelation to men. Objects were seen as in a dream, whether men were asleep (Isa. 29:7; Dan. 2:19, 28; 4:9; 7:1-2, 7, 13; 8:18), in a trance with their eyes open (Num. 24:4, 16; Acts 10:10; 11:5; 22:17), in deep meditation (Jer. 23:16), in prayer (Dan. 9:21-24; 10:2-21), or in the course of duty while awake (Isa. 6; Ezek. 1:1; 8:3; 40:2;

43:3; Mat. 17:1-9; Lk. 1:22; 24:23; Acts 9:10-12; 10:3, 17-19; 12:9; Rev. 1:10; 4:1-2). Whether one was asleep or awake when he saw a vision, the image or picture came to the mind, and the message of God was always clear. Whatever was predicted always happened or will yet happen in accordance with the vision. Both visions and dreams are referred to as means of revelation from God (Joel 2:28; Acts 2:17)."

The fact that Paul did not know if he was given this revelation while being in his body or out of it proves he may have been raptured in his natural body just like Enoch (Gen. 5:24), Elijah (2 Ki. 2), Philip (Acts 8:39), and John (Rev.4:1). He was a learned man and had complete faith as to the possibility of actually being taken to heaven, though it is certain he didn't know about John's rapture since the two events were about 50 years apart, and that of Paul's rapture being before John's. While it cannot be proven that Paul had an actual rapture, it also cannot be disproved. Verse 2 lets us know that he was "caught up," which is the same language used in 1 Thessalonians 4:16-17. My belief is that he was actually there in heaven to receive a revelation from God, which is exactly what happened with John.

NATURAL BODY
JOHN

After this I looked, and, behold, a door *was* opened in heaven: and the first voice which I heard *was* as it were of a trumpet talking with me; which said, Come up hither, and I will shew thee things which must be hereafter. 2 And immediately I was in the spirit: and, behold, a throne was set in heaven, and *one* sat on the throne (Rev. 4:1-2).

John was a beloved disciple and apostle of Jesus. He was the youngest of the twelve and the longest living original disciple. Tradition holds that John was about 100 years old when he died in Ephesus and had been saved from the physical death of boiling oil like Shadrach, Meshach, and Abednego were saved from the burning fiery furnace (Dan. 3). According to Tertullian (in The Prescription of Heretics) John was banished (presumably to Patmos) after being plunged into boiling oil in Rome and suffering nothing from it. It is said that all in the audience of Colosseum were converted to Christianity upon witnessing this miracle.

This rapture occurred while John was banished to the Isle of Patmos (Rev. 1:9), a volcanic, treeless, rocky island about 6 x 10 miles, 30 miles southwest of Samos. It was made a place of exile by the Romans for the lowest of criminals. There is no doubt that John was bodily taken to heaven, because the Lord actually told John to "come up hither" (Rev. 4:1), and a door was opened in heaven, which was a real opening to heaven. This opening was translated from the Greek: *thura* (GSN-<G2374>), which is a portal or entrance; door; gate. The same thing happens in Revelation 19:11 right before God and the armies of heaven, made up of all glorified saints and faithful angels, come back from heaven to earth.

I used to wonder how long it would take the saints to travel from earth to heaven after the rapture of the church. I have seen videos made of Jesus' view as He travels through space and past planets to get to the atmosphere of earth in order to call up the church. Likewise, I contemplated the time it would take the armies of heaven to ride their horses through space to fight in Armageddon and take back the earth.

I considered that the whole world would be able to see Jesus' return because of His great and glorious light He gives off in space. I also contemplated that if Jesus and the glorious church were taking a straight path to earth, then it would take at least 24 hours of travel to make that journey. At that rate the earth's rotation would travel full circle, and all would be able to look up in the night sky and see this cloud of witnesses shining bright at His return. These are all great ponderings of curiosity, but the simple truth has always been in Scripture. There is a door, or portal, that opens up in the sky, or just outside the earth's atmosphere, and we shall go through it as John did in Revelation 4:1.

NATURAL BODY
ISRAEL AT THE SECOND COMING

We have just concluded all natural bodied raptures of the righteous through Scripture. There are still two more scriptural raptures that will take place of natural people in the future. These raptures result in no glorification of the body and are exclusive only to those who are found worthy to enter into the Millennial Kingdom. All true Israelites, or the Jewish people, will be transported from their places around the world back to Israel at the time of the Second Coming.

> <u>Immediately after the tribulation of those days</u> shall the sun be darkened, and the moon shall not give her light, and the stars shall fall from heaven, and the powers of the heavens shall be shaken: And then shall appear the sign of the Son of man in heaven: and then shall all the tribes of the earth mourn, and <u>they shall see the Son of man coming in the clouds of heaven</u> with power and great glory. And he shall send his angels <u>with a great sound of a trumpet</u>, and <u>they shall gather together his elect from the four winds</u>, from one end of heaven to the other (Mat. 24:29-31).

The passage of Matthew 24:29-31 is often used as a pillar for proof of a post-tribulation rapture, but I'll show you that it is only proof for a rapture of a specific race of natural people at the Second Coming. From this passage we see that actual angels will be sent to literally gather Israel. Another passage tells of another purpose for the angels at that same time. They will also separate the tares from the wheat (Mat. 13:38-50). The tares and wheat separation is the same as the judgment of the nations (Mat. 25:31-46). The angels who come to earth with Jesus (2 Thess. 1:7-10) will be the ones transporting many people from their places on earth to their destination before the King of all kings at His coming.

How fast this event will be for man is not stated, but if an angel can fly as fast as the speed of light, then he can travel around the equator of the earth seven times in a single second. If travel time is at the speed of thought, then travel time of transporting a person from one place to another will be even faster. If the angels are riding spirit horses from heaven, then it may take longer, giving the transported humans a scary experience, as they would then have time to know what is going on. There are horses in God's army that angels have ridden in times past. Jesus and the saints will also ride these heavenly beasts at the Second Coming (2 Ki. 2:11-12; 6:13-17; Zech. 1:8-11; 6:1-8; Rev. 19:11-21).

The proof that the angels are gathering Jews to bring them to their land of Israel comes from Matthew 24:31, where it is written that the angels will gather the elect at the trumpet sound. Trumpets were always blown for the purpose of gathering Israel (Ex. 19:13-19; Lev. 25:9; 1 Sam. 13:3; 2 Sam. 2:28). This trumpet is not one of the trumpets blown during the first half of the Tribulation sounding for judgment (Rev. 8:2, 6), nor is it the trumpet sound to call up the church and all resurrected saints to heaven (1 Thess. 4:16; 1 Cor. 15:51-54; Rev. 4:1). This trumpet is predicted in Isaiah.

> All ye inhabitants of the world, and dwellers on the earth, see ye, when he lifteth up an ensign on the mountains; and when he bloweth a trumpet, hear ye (Isa. 18:3). And it shall come to pass in that day, *that* the great trumpet shall be blown, and they shall come which were ready to perish in the land of Assyria, and the outcasts in the land of Egypt, and shall worship the LORD in the holy mount at Jerusalem (Isa. 27:13).

The prophet Zechariah foretells the same trumpet that is blown before the angels gather the elect (Zech. 9:14). But who are the elect of Matthew 24:31? The word elect simply means chosen. Any individual or group of individuals who have been chosen by God would be God's elect. In the case of Matthew 24, the elect are Jewish, as the entire chapter is completely Jewish in nature.

According to Scripture, there are four individuals or groups of individuals that have been called the elect: Christ (Isa. 42:1; 1 Pet. 2:6), Christians (Rom. 8:33; Col. 3:12; Tit. 1:1; Jn. 15:16; Eph. 1:4; 2:10; 2 Thess. 2:13; 2 Jn. 1:1, 13), Israel (Isa. 45:4; 65:9, 22; Mat. 24:21-31; Mk. 13:22, 27; 1 Pet. 1:2), and angels (1 Tim. 5:21). So it is faulty to prove a post-tribulation rapture based upon the elect being gathered by the angels in Matthew 24:29-31. That conclusion is solely based upon the church being the elect spoken of, when that word is never used solely for the church.

Would it not be more reasonable to believe the language of Matthew 24 was directly speaking about the Jewish elect being brought back to Israel since this has been predicted? Matthew 24:31 even states that the elect will be gathered from the four winds, which is exactly what Isaiah and Moses say will happen in "that day."

> And it shall come to pass in that day, *that* the Lord shall set his hand again the second time to <u>recover the remnant of his people</u>, which shall be left, from Assyria, and from Egypt, and from Pathros, and from Cush, and from Elam, and from Shinar, and from Hamath, and from the islands of the sea. And he shall set up an ensign for the nations, <u>and shall assemble the outcasts of Israel, and gather together the dispersed of Judah</u> from the four corners of the earth (Isa. 11:11-12). If *any* of thine be driven out unto the outmost *parts* of heaven, from thence will the LORD thy God gather thee, and from thence will he fetch thee (Dt. 30:4).

The "four corners of the earth" simply mean the four directions of the earth (Isa. 11:11-12; Mat. 24:31; Rev. 7:1-3; 20:8). Simply put, the Jewish people will be raptured in natural bodies from around the earth in order to be gathered before their Messiah in their God-given land of Israel, whose borders will be greatly expanded compared to what the maps of today claim (Gen. 15:18).

NATURAL BODY PEOPLE FOUND TO BE SHEEP AT THE JUDGMENT OF NATIONS AT THE SECOND COMING

The last company of righteous, natural men to be translated from one place to another will be the sheep at the Judgment of Nations at the Second Coming (Mat. 25:31-46). Just as the angels will gather the Jewish elect in that day to bring them to their land, in like manner, the angels also gather the people for this judgment, bringing them before

Jesus to see if they are fit to enter His Millennial Reign. This happens directly after the Second Coming. Exactly when in chronological sequence is not stated. The angels may gather the Jewish people to Israel before this, or even at the same time.

This judgment is on the gentile nations (Mat. 25:32), immediately after the Seven Year Tribulation (Mat. 24:29-31). The place is in Israel, where Jesus lands (Zech. 14; Mat. 25:31; Rev. 19:11-21). Some will be destroyed, while others will be preserved to enter into the thousand-year Dispensation of Divine Government (Mat. 13:41-50; 24:51; 25:34, 41, 46; Zech. 14; Isa. 53; Joel 3). The judgment is on the basis of their treatment of Christ's brethren, the Jews during the soon, future tribulation (Mat. 25:31-46). These are Jesus' brethren according to the flesh (Mat. 10:6; 25:40; Jn. 1:11; Rom. 9:5), not according to the adoption into God's family (Rom. 8:14-25; 1 Jn. 3:1-3). The guilty are referred to as goats, while the innocent are referred to as sheep (Mat. 13:39-50; 25:32-33).

This judgment will determine who is worthy of entrance into the Kingdom of Heaven and who will be executed and cut off from entrance into the kingdom. Many say no one is worthy, only Jesus (Rev. 5:1-5), but this is not true across the board. Jesus is the only one worthy to break the seals and open the book (Rev. 5; Rev. 10), but He reveal that man can be worthy, lest He gave a worthless and meaningless command to pray that we will be counted worthy to escape the things coming on the face of the earth and to stand before the Son of man (Lk. 21:34-36). That is a direct reference to the pre-tribulation rapture, and worthiness there comes through believing Jesus is who the Bible says He is and a total forsaking of sin (Mat. 7:13-14, 21-23; 15:10-20; 19:17; Jn. 8:31-36; 14:15-24; 15:1-18; 1 Jn. 2:1-6; Rev. 2:5, 16; 3:3, 19).

This Judgment of Nations is not based directly on this. Worthiness to enter the kingdom of heaven at the beginning of the Millennial Reign is simply based on how one treated the Jewish people. Daniel 12:12 will then be fulfilled when we are told, "Blessed is he that waiteth, and cometh to the thousand three hundred and five and thirty days," which is the actual day of the proclamation of the kingdom. This is seventy-five days after the nations will be gathered and judged. The Jews will have already bene regathered and settled in the land of promise, and all essential preliminary preparations for the kingdom will be made.

The natural, living people who enter the Millennial Kingdom will repopulate the earth for eternal generations (Gen. 1:26-28; 8:22; 9:12; Ps. 127:3; Isa. 9:6-7; 59:21; Dan. 2:44-45; 7:13-14, 27; Lk. 1:3-33; Rev. 11:15; 22:4-5). The eternal kingdom of God will have two separate and distinct types of human-beings: natural man and glorified man. Glorified man will be flesh and bone like Jesus in an immortal and incorruptible body and be ruler of all creation (1 Thess. 4:16-17; 1 Cor. 15:51-54; 2 Tim. 2:12; Heb. 12:28; Rev. 1:6; 2:26-27; 3:21), while natural man will be the subjects of the kingdom, be flesh and blood, and will also be immortal as long as they do not rebel against God's commandments and eternal laws throughout the Millennium or at the end of the thousand years with Satan's last ditch attempt to overthrow God (Dan. 7:9-14, 18, 22, 27; Zech. 14:16-21; Isa. 2:1-4; 9:6-7; Mat. 25:31-46; Rev. 11:15; 20:4-6; 22:4-5).

I need to be clear, Matthew 25:32 says He will judge all nations, but this will not include every person in all nations, because not all people on earth will know Jesus has returned to earth, or even who Jesus is for that matter (Isa. 2; 99:19-21).

Thus saith the LORD of hosts; <u>In those days</u> *it shall come to pass*, that ten men shall take hold out of all languages of the nations, even shall take hold of the skirt of him <u>that is a Jew</u>, saying, <u>We will go with you</u>: for we have <u>heard</u> *that* <u>God *is* with you</u> (Zech. 8:23).

Not all will be raptured (transported from one place to another by supernatural means) from their place on earth to be judged by Jesus who will be in Israel. It will be an individual judgment of all involved with Israel when Christ comes to set up His kingdom, not a judgment of the wicked dead, which is the Great White Throne Judgment at the end of the Millennial Reign by God the Father (Rev. 20:1-15).

Clearly, not all people alive on earth will be raptured to Israel, for you have just read in Zechariah 8:23 that many will go to Israel to see God for themselves. Why would people who have been transported to Israel say they will go with you (a Jew), for they have heard (not seen) that God is there reigning? The time of the judgment of the nations will make people truly understand Genesis 12:1-3, where God promises Abraham that He will curse or bless people according to how they treat Israel, and show how Christ will give the meek the earth as promised (Ps. 37:11; Mat. 5:5).

As Zechariah 8:23 expresses, "In those days" the Messiah Jesus will reign and become known to the uttermost parts of the entire earth, even in the tribes deep in the Amazon where Jesus still has not been known. You say, "How can this be?" I know the common belief is that all on earth will see Christ and His saints and angels in the sky at the Second Coming, but this is not in harmony with the whole of Scripture (Zech. 8:23; 14:16-21; Isa. 2:2-4; Mic. 4).

When Scripture says every eye will see Him, it must be understood that this is referring to the Jerusalem area where He opens up the portal to lead His army from heaven to earth (Rev. 19:11).

> Behold, he cometh with clouds; and every eye shall see him, and they *also* which pierced him: and all kindreds of the earth shall wail because of him. Even so, Amen (Rev. 1:7).

The armies of the nations are the ones that will be surrounding Jerusalem when Christ comes (Zech. 14:1-5; Mat. 24:29-31). So all beliefs that the invention of the television is how Revelation 1:7 will be fulfilled is inaccurate, proving further that the rapture of the sheep and goats will not include every person from all nations, just those involved in the treatment of the Jewish people during the Tribulation.

It will take a bit of time for the information to be known everywhere that God is now ruling on earth, a change has taken place in world governments, and Christ, David, the apostles, and resurrected saints are taking them over (Zech. 14:1-21; Isa. 9:6-7; Lk. 1:32-33; Rev. 11:15; 20:1-10). This process could take weeks, months or years to bring all people under the submission of the kingdom of heaven on earth, but this is the main purpose of the thousand-year period on earth. The saints and Christ will be publishing the new laws, bringing about universal peace and prosperity, and put all enemies under foot, ridding the whole earth of all rebels against God and His authority (Isa. 65:20; 1 Cor. 15:24-28; Eph. 1:10; Rev. 11:15; 20:1-10).

GLORIFIED AND ETERNAL BODY
JESUS

With a cloud of many eye witnesses, Jesus Christ did rise from death. He is alive! Heaven will be emptied out of all saints, whether they are spirits, natural bodied men, or glorified people. This must take place in order to begin the next phase of redemption for earth and man. There is a resurrection, and if a resurrection, then a rapture, for the plan of God cannot wait till all in Christ die, for there will always be the righteous of the earth. The first resurrection must have raptures of not only the dead, but also the living, so that some will not see death, but just be changed to immortality and transported from earth to heaven.

> For I delivered unto you first of all that which I also received, how that Christ died for our sins according to the scriptures; And that he was buried, and that he rose again the third day according to the scriptures: And that he was seen of Cephas, then of the twelve: After that, he was seen of above five hundred brethren at once; of whom the greater part remain unto this present, but some are fallen asleep. After that, he was seen of James; then of all the apostles. And last of all he was seen of me also, as of one born out of due time (1 Cor. 15:3-8).

> And *that* he died for all, that they which live should not henceforth live unto themselves, but unto him which died for them, and rose again (2 Cor.5:15).

> Now if Christ be preached that he rose from the dead, how say some among you that there is no resurrection of the dead (1 Cor. 15:12)?

> For to this end Christ both died, and rose, and revived, that he might be Lord both of the dead and living (Rom. 14:9).

> For if we believe that Jesus died and rose again, even so them also which sleep in Jesus will God bring with him (1 Thess. 4:14).

Even though the resurrection of Christ is the greatest news in the Christian faith due to it being an essential belief of a person's salvation (1 Cor. 15:1-4), we will begin this journey of rapture teaching with the first substantial rapture in all of Scripture. Jesus is the first fruits of the resurrection (1 Cor. 15:20, 23), but He is is also the first rapture in the first resurrection.

None of the natural bodied raptures are as significant as the ones in the first resurrection. To remind you, the first resurrection has five parts, beginning with Christ two thousand years ago and ending with the two witnesses at the end of the Seven Year Tribulation. The plan and reasoning beyond the five Bible raptures of natural men were divinely orchestrated, but lack the hope and substance that all believers have regarding the raptures in the first resurrection.

The raptures of Enoch, Elijah, Philip, Paul, and John resulted in a continued life in a mortal body. Our hope is in the glorified body that is like Christ's body (Phil. 3:21; 1 Jn. 3:2). The first resurrection is not a resurrection of all involved, for the living "in Christ," and the 144,000 will be changed, not resurrected from the dead. But, the first resurrection will include a rapture of absolutely everyone involved, for all will go to heaven after they put on immortality of their physical bodies.

Enoch and Elijah were raptured to heaven and will return when the Antichrist breaks covenant with Israel, ceases the sacrifices in their newly built temple, and declares himself to be God (Dan. 9:24-27). These two men have an important mission, but they were not a part of the first resurrection, which is the blessed hope for the Christians who have forsaken sin to follow Jesus (Eph. 5:27; Tit. 2:11-13).

Philip was raptured only a couple dozen miles away, which is substantial for a day with nothing faster than a horse to ride, yet he was on foot. Philip wasn't even taken to heaven. His rapture was essential and purposed, but not a changing of his mortal body to be like Christ's (Phil. 3:21). Paul and John had amazing revelations given to them in heaven, but also came back to earth, lived their days, then died their appointed death (Heb. 9:27).

To bring the significance home, I'll just say that no rapture was pointless, but not all raptures are crucial to the faith and plan of God for man. Do you know how exciting it was for Enoch and Elijah to be raptured to the throne of God for all these thousands of years (Zech. 4:14)? Yet, they also await their resurrection and rapture to be redeemed from their mortal bodies to put on immortality and have a body like Jesus (1 Jn. 3:2-3; Rev. 11:7-12). Glorification is one of the phases of salvation, which is a change of realm and a new dominion with God (Rom. 8:17, 30; Acts 3:13; Phil. 3:21; 1 Cor. 15:21-58; Rev. 5:10; 20:1-7). All righteous souls, even in heaven, are awaiting the fullness of their salvation, even though they are eternally saved.

We believers on earth await for more of our salvation in its many different aspects and phases, but it will not be a guarantee for the righteous on earth during this age until the end of a life ending in holiness. Here are several other sample scriptures that reveal eternal life is not an eternal possession now and will not be until the end of a life of holiness, because people have to continue to the end to be saved: Dan. 12:2; Mat. 7:13-14; 12:31-32; 19:28-29; 25:46; Mk. 10:29-30; 16:15;

Lk. 18:9-30; Jn. 5:28; Acts 5:3, 32; 7:51; Rom. 2:7; 5:21; 6:21-23; 1 Cor. 3:16-17; 6:9-10; Gal. 6:7-8; 1 Tim. 1:16; 4:8; 6:12, 19; Tit. 1:2; 3:7; Heb. 6:4-6; 10:26-29; 1 Pet. 1:5, 9, 13; 3:7; 1 Jn. 2:25; Jude 20-24; Rev. 2:5, 16; 3:3, 15-16, 19; etc.

Jesus' rapture to heaven is by far the best rapture that has ever taken place, but is just the beginning phase of the rapture of all the saints from now until the end of the soon coming Tribulation. All saints from man's beginning to the end of this Age of Grace (at the end of the Great Tribulation) will be the rulers of the eternal subjects of earth throughout eternity. This has to be an amazing time-span to live in. Even though man sees 6,000 years as forever, it is only a short time compared to eternity. The down side to this time-span is that there is equally much to lose, equivalent only to the good news of there being so much to gain.

Yes, this time of testing you live offers so much loss or reward, and the only way to compare the two is by how eternally and far stretched the two rewards are from each other. Choose this day who you will serve and keep your eyes fixed onto Him at all costs (Dt. 30:11-16). To look to the left or the right is to take your eyes off Jesus and onto the world. Like Peter walking on the water, you will fall (Jas. 4:4-8; 1 Jn. 2:15-17).

Most believe Jesus was raptured 40 days after He rose from the grave, which is true. This is only one rapture of Christ's since His resurrection. Jesus was also transported to the lower parts of inner earth and back to the surface of the earth three days later at His resurrection (Mat. 12:40; 27:53-54; Eph. 4:8-10). That was only a transportation of His spirit and soul. Little known fact, He also went to heaven and came back after His resurrection (Jn. 20:17-19), well before the commonly known rapture of the 40 days. The well-known rapture of Jesus at the end of the 40 days was His return to heaven, leading the many resurrected men, and souls and spirits of just men whose bodies were not resurrected (Mat. 27:53-54; Acts 1:9-11; Eph. 4:8-10; Heb. 12:23).

This is exciting! Let's look at the scriptural message given showing how Jesus went to heaven and then actually came back to earth for many weeks. This information from the Book of Matthew is scarcely known.

> *Jesus saith unto her, Mary. She turned herself, and saith unto him, Rabboni; which is to say, Master. Jesus saith unto her, Touch me not; for I am not yet ascended to my Father: but go to my brethren, and say unto them, I ascend unto my Father, and your Father; and to my God, and your God. Mary Magdalene came and told the disciples that she had seen the Lord, and that he had spoken these things unto her. Then the same day at evening, being the first day of the week, when the doors were shut where the disciples were assembled for fear of the Jews, came Jesus and stood in the midst, and saith unto them, Peace be unto you. And when he had so said, he shewed unto them his hands and his side. Then were the disciples glad, when they saw the Lord. Then said Jesus to them again, Peace be unto you: as my Father hath sent me, even so send I you (Mat. 20:16-21).*

Mary attempted to hold Him and Jesus said, "Touch me not," that is, "Do not cling to Me. I am going immediately to heaven. Go tell My brethren that I ascend to God but will be back again to see them." Despite many theories of why Jesus could not be touched before going to heaven to present Himself before the Father, Matthew 28:9 shows that He was touched by His disciple, though this was after He had told Mary not to touch Him.

The key is not that He could not be touched, but that He was not to be detained, because He was going directly to see His Father. That very day, as John 20:19 says, He did ascend to heaven and came back to appear to His disciples. This was a rapture to heaven and back to earth, before He ascended 40 days after His resurrection in Acts 1:9-11.

There are so many in Christendom who forsake the teaching of the pre-tribulation rapture because they claim there are only two comings of Christ from heaven, not three. They say it is called the Second Coming, which would actually be the third coming if He came at least seven years prior. Well, the "Second Coming" is merely a doctrinal term like the Millennial Reign, or the trinity. Scripture never states that Jesus will only come to earth two times.

The truth is there are two separate and distinct comings of Christ out of heaven in the future that we can call a coming of the Lord. One is before the Tribulation when He comes from heaven to the clouds surrounding the earth to rapture all the dead and living in Christ. He doesn't even come to earth at that coming. He will then take them to heaven to live with Him and His Father and all others who dwell in heaven (Jn. 14:1-3; Lk. 21:34-36; 1 Cor. 15:23, 51-54; Eph. 5:27; Phil. 3:21; Col. 3:4; 1 Thess. 4:13-18; 5:1-11; Thess. 2:7-8; Jas. 5:7-8; 1 Jn. 3:1-3).

Another coming from heaven is the Second Coming to the earth, and not to the clouds only. The purpose of this coming is to bring all the raptured saints from heaven with Him to fight at Armageddon and set up the kingdom of heaven in this world (Zech. 14:5; Mat. 24:29-31; 2 Thess. 1:7-10; Jude 1:14-15; Rev. 19:11-21). To further prove the faulty thinking of those who only believe in two comings, Jesus actually came back to earth after He was resurrected and raptured, as we have just read from John 20:16-21. With all sober mindedness of thinking, no one would say the Second

Coming happened when Jesus descended back to earth the day He was resurrected.

Not only that, but many Old Testament scriptures prove Jesus was on earth on many occasions. He was referred to as an angel, though not really an angel at all, but the second person of the trinity. This was a physical appearance of God. In many passages He is called "the angel of God," "the angel of the Lord," "His angel," "Mine angel," and "the angel of His presence." (Gen. 16:7-14; 21:11-18; 22:12; 31:11-13; 32:24-30; 48:15-16; Ex. 3:1-6 cp. with Acts 7:30-38; Ex. 13:21-22; 14:19-20 cp. with Ps. 34:7 and Ps. 35:1-6; Ex. 14:19 cp. with Heb. 13:21; Ex. 23:20-23 cp. with Ex. 32:34 and Num. 20:16 and Isa. 63:9; Num. 22; Judges 2:1-5; 6; 13; 17:6; Zech. 1:7-17; etc.). Jesus was also referred to as an angel in Revelation 8:3-5; 10:1 – 11:3.

"Angel" means messenger of God, so the term has been used by many messengers of God, even when these messengers have not been angelic beings. Revelation 1:20; 2:1, 8, 12, 18; 3:1, 7, 14; 19:9-10 use the word angel for men. When the text makes it clear that these angels are not angelic beings, such as in the above, then the language and meaning will be evident on whom they are referring (Jesus, men, or angelic beings). Angelic beings can clearly be understood with many text (Matthew 1:20, 24; 2:13, 19; 28:2-7; Lk. 1:11-38; 2:9-14; Acts 5:19-20; 8:26; 12:7-23). So it must be understood now that the proof of no pre-tribulation rapture due to the doctrinal term "Second Coming" is a fruitless argument.

Several things are taught about the resurrected body when analyzing the text concerning Jesus. He had been raised to life in His resurrected body, as the tomb was empty (Mat. 28:5-7), and went to heaven and back before He showed His disciple the holes in His hands, feet, and side. Many people, even a pastor friend of mine, believe Jesus does not bear the holes in His body any more. I believe His thinking is that, though Jesus was raised bodily, He was not glorified in His eternal body until entering heaven. I suppose It's just too far a stretch for some I suppose to believe God could have any imperfection in His body.

I tell you the truth, Jesus will reign eternal generations of natural people continuously born throughout eternity (Mat. 13:39-50; 25:46; Rev. 20:7-10; 22:1-2). All will see what He did for them, even to a million generations away. After all, Jesus did go to heaven before He showed His disciples His pierced body (Lk. 24:39). Was He not yet in a glorified body, or can a natural man walk through walls (Jn. 20:19)? Yes, Jesus was in a resurrected body that was glorified and immortal (Mk. 16:19; Lk. 24:39, 51; Acts 1:11). He walked through walls (or a door) and had already ascended to heaven and back (Jn. 20:17), still with His holes in His hands and side.

The practical application for us is that a normal person, like you and me, will not have an eternal monument in our body to show future generations what it took to save them from hell, so all our bodily imperfections will be healed. We will also be able to eat, walk through material objects like Jesus, and be able to appear and disappear, or be visible and invisible at the speed of thought. Travel would more than likely be at the speed of thought with no hindrance of distance.

After all, the resurrected saints will have a home in the heavenly city, the New Jerusalem, the capital of heaven (Jn. 14:1-3), yet we will be ruling and reigning on earth with Christ (Dan. 7:18, 27; 1 Cor. 6:2-4). I'm sure the doctrine of the rapture (being transported from one place to another) will not be so unbelievable during the thousand-year reign with Christ. The glorified saints will be commuting, what could be millions of miles, to and from work every day. Makes my one hour trip each way to work not seem so bad. But I drive 75 mph in a car, not at the speed of thought in a glorified body.

GLORIFIED AND ETERNAL BODY MANY OLD TESTAMENT SAINTS FROM ABRAHAM'S BOSOM

As discussed in the resurrection section, Jesus was in a chamber in hell called Abraham's Bosom (Lk. 16:22), or paradise (Lk. 23:43). This was a very safe, comforting, dwelling place for the souls and spirits of the righteous who had died before the cross. Jesus had to go there to set those captives of Satan free. Satan had legal right to hold them because their sins were not taken away, just covered and declared righteous (Gen. 15:6; Rom. 4:3, 6; Gal. 3:6; Heb. 2:14-15; Jas. 2:23; 1 Jn. 3:5-7). Jesus also proclaimed a message to the bound angels in another chamber in hell, called tarsus, who sinned in the days of Noah (1 Pt. 3:19; cp. with Gen. 6:4; 2 Pt. 2:4; Jude 1:6-7).

When Jesus fulfilled His mission in lower earth (Mat. 12:40), He brought up all the righteous, emptying the chamber in hell called Abraham's Bosom. Many bodies of Old Testament saints were raised when their graves were opened (Mat. 27:52-53; Eph. 4:8-10), and all the rest of the saved souls and spirits not yet given resurrected bodies were released from captivity. Now all dead in Christ go directly to heaven since all their sins were washed away by the death, burial, and resurrection of Christ (Micah 7:19; 1 Cor. 15:1-4; 2 Cor. 5:8; Eph. 4:8-10; Phil. 1:21-24; Heb. 12:23).

So our focus rapture of people here in their eternal body takes place when Jesus ascended to heaven on the 40th day after their resurrection. He took captivity captive with Him when He ascended on high (Eph. 4:8-10; Heb. 2:14-

15). They had been walking the earth, showing themselves to many for 40 days, but they did in fact ascend at the same time as Jesus, some glorified in eternal bodies, others still await the resurrection from among the dead.

Scripture lacks detail in telling why some were resurrected and not all, but one theory I have is that only the graves in proximity of Christ's were opened to allow the resurrected saints to come out (Mat. 27:52-53). I have heard many times the theory that if Jesus did not say Lazarus' name when calling him out of the grave, that all graves in proximity of His voice would have opened. Perhaps the resurrecting power that glorified Jesus' mortal and dead body to life and immortality had a larger diameter than just His tomb alone. We will find out soon.

GLORIFIED AND ETERNAL BODY EVERY PERSON IN CHRIST AT HIS COMING FOR THE SAINTS BEFORE THE TRIBULATION

It's been a long time coming, but you finally made it to the most commonly understood rapture of them all. This rapture needs no introduction, reigning as the undisputed, the most debated end-time doctrine of all time, the rapture of the church!

> For the Lord himself shall descend from heaven with a shout, with the voice of the archangel, and with the trump of God: and the dead in Christ shall rise first: Then we which are alive *and* remain shall be caught up together with them in the clouds, to meet the Lord in the air: and so shall we ever be with the Lord (1 Thess. 4:16-17).

More verses included: (Lk. 21:34-36; Jn. 14:1-3; 1 Cor. 15:23, 51-54; 2 Cor. 5:1-8; Eph. 5:7; Phil. 3:11, 20-21; Col. 3:4; 1 Thess. 2:19; 3:13; 4:13-17; 5:9, 23; 2 Thess. 2:1, 7; Jas. 5:7-8; 1 Pet. 5:4; 1 Jn. 2:28; 3:2). Everyone on earth and in Christ, dead or alive, will be translated at this time. Not a single person will be forgotten and left behind who is in Christ at that great trumpet blast (1 Cor. 15:51-54; 1 Thess. 4:16-17; Rev. 4:1).

Speaking of that trumpet sound, there is a belief that the whole world will know the rapture happened because the trumpet sound will be heard by all and there will be opened graves from all who are in Christ. Now, I can't biblically dispute what is not clearly presented with certain detail. What I do know is that the graves do not have to open for people to go through the dirt, or whatever is over their decaying body. Jesus' tomb was open, yet He could walk through walls (Jn. 20:16-21). The many who were resurrected with Him had their graves opened (Mat. 27:52-53), but they were still able to go through material substances like Christ.

If the trumpet is heard by all, then it will be explained away as alien in origin due to the great deception following the rapture (2 Thess. 2:1-12). The only thing I know for sure is there will be some freaked out people who have a dead body around them, such as hospitals, morgues, etc. that just disappears in front of them. One sad thing is that some will be at a showing at a funeral where the body remains and later have understanding that it means that loved one is in hell. The good news is there will still be hope for the living at that time, so those left behind must let the dead go and choose life through Jesus.

So this rapture, often called the rapture of the church, will be the most notable rapture of them all due to the millions that will vanish from around the world. As for the living in Christ, this is the rapture of the church only, but the rapture also includes all saints from Able (1 Thess. 4:16-17), through to the thief on the cross (Lk. 23:43), all who died in the Old Testament days, before the death of Jesus on Calvary. Even though they are living painless, fully conscious lives in the presence of God Almighty, they are still anxiously awaiting the resurrection (2 Cor. 5:8).

Those are some of the ones who will come back with Jesus to be resurrected and raptured (1 Thess. 3:13; 4:13-15), where all saints on earth will then meet the Lord in the air (1 Thess. 4:16-17; 1 Cor. 15:51-54). The rest of the saints come back from heaven with Jesus so they can be resurrected. They are saints from the church age that have already died. Old Testament saints are not the church, just like the future tribulation saints are not part of the church. So the term "Rapture of the Church" is true, but lacking some detail concerning all who will be a part of this highly anticipated rapture.

Even with all the contention this rapture stirs among the brethren, the timing of this rapture is undoubtedly before the Seven Year Tribulation. Proving the entire doctrine of the pre-tribulation rapture is a book all on its own, so I will only make a few facts clear. It would be an overload of information for the main purpose of this book, which is to educate people on the reality of the raptures and resurrections through Scripture, showing that all will be a part of one of the raptures and resurrections no matter what the condition of their soul at death.

The proof of a pre-tribulation is being sprinkled throughout this book and will be addressed thoroughly in book 2, but the most overwhelming teaching of the timing of the rapture of the church is from Revelation.

> <u>After this</u> I looked, and, behold, a door *was* opened in heaven: and the first voice which I heard *was* as it were of a trumpet talking with me; which said, <u>Come up hither</u>, and I will <u>shew thee things which must be hereafter</u> (Rev. 4:1).

Those who oppose of this doctrine say this tells nothing of the rapture of anyone except for John, who was simply caught up before the throne of God (Rev. 4:2) to see many things in heaven (Rev. 4:1 – 5:14).

This passage combined with Revelation 1:19 shows very simply that the rapture of the church is indeed in Revelation 4:1. If not here, then where is the rapture in Revelation? Could it be that the most revealing end-time book is void of such an anticipated and soon to be historic event? Absolutely not! Revelation 1:19 truly is the key to understanding the sequence of the book of Revelation. Notice the three divisions of the book.

> Write the things which thou hast seen, and the things which are, and the things which shall be hereafter (Rev. 1:19).

1) The things which thou hast seen
2) The things which are
3) The things which shall be hereafter

There are three main sections to the Book of Revelation. Chapter 1 speaks of the things which John did see in the vision of Christ in the midst of the candlesticks (Rev. 1:12-20). Next, John was told to write the things which are, which is the church age (Rev. 2-3). John saw this revelation in 95

– 96 A.D., and the church was established more than sixty years prior. Also, the whole book is addressed to the seven churches in Asia Minor, which have a prophetical application to also symbolize the entire church age (Rev. 1:3), as well as an individual application to everyone living in this church age as proved by the endings of all seven letters by saying, "He that overcomes..." (Rev. 2:7, 11, 17, 26; 3:5, 12, 21).

Now if you'll notice Revelation 4:1 again, it begins with "After this," and ends with "I will shew thee things which must be hereafter." After what? It can only be the events after the rapture of the church (Rev. 4:1 - Rev. 22:5). These include the scenes in heaven (Rev. 4 - Rev. 5), which does show a gap of time in between the rapture (Rev. 4:1) and the beginning of the Tribulation (Rev. 6:1), which lasts for seven years (Dan. 9:27; 2 Thess. 2:7-12; Rev. 6:1 – Rev. 19:21), yet the gap agreed upon my many end-time prophecy students and teachers is unknown. The gap will only be a few days long, up to two months. No definite time is given, but biblically speaking, it could be years. Book 3 has extensive research pointing to a short period of time in the gap. The seven seals and their parenthetical content are in Revelation 4:1 - Rev. 19:21, the Millennium is in Revelation 20, and the new heaven and new earth are taught in Revelation 21:1 - Rev. 22:5, while Revelation 22:6-21 conclude the events.

If the things beyond Revelation 4:1 must be after the things of the churches (Rev. 2 – Rev. 3), then they will not be fulfilled along with the things of the churches. This means that every event of Revelation 4 - Revelation 22 must be fulfilled after the rapture of the church. It also means that no historical or present event could possibly be a fulfillment of any event of Revelation 4 - Revelation 22, though many are trying to say some of the seals have been broken and some of the trumpets have been blown by the angels. Some even claim the woman of Revelation 12 is Mary and the man child is Jesus being born, Who was later caught up to be with God in heaven (Rev. 12:1-5). It must be understood that the rapture of the church is in Revelation 4:1, preceding all the events of the Tribulation (Rev. 4:1 – Rev. 19:21), or Daniels 70th Week (Dan. 9:24-27). The church is never mentioned past Revelation 3 for a reason.

GLORIFIED AND ETERNAL BODY THE 144,000 JEWS IN THE MIDDLE OF THE TRIBULATION

The 144,000 will be raptured (caught up) in the middle of the Seven Year Tribulation, making the third of five exclusive raptures in the first resurrection beginning with Jesus. They will be two groups out of the five raptures that has no resurrection. Just like the rapture of the living in Christ at the beginning of the Tribulation (Daniel's 70th Week), the 144,000 Jews from Revelation 7:1-8 will be living on earth at the time God calls them up (Rev. 12:5). They will be saved by believing and following Jesus as their Messiah after the rapture of the church, for no righteous person will be left on earth at the time of the pre-tribulation rapture, including children under their age of being held accountable (Mat. 18:1-10; 19:14). The exact age of accountability is not known. It may be different for everyone.

The 144,000 are the man child of Revelation 12:5, which says, "And she brought forth a _man child_, who was to rule all nations with a rod of iron: and her child was <u>caught up</u> unto God, and _to his throne_." To prove they are the man child of Revelation 12:5, let's first just be honest with clear language and agree that whoever the man child is, he will be undoubtedly caught up, which is the same language used for the rapture of the Old Testament saints and church in 1 Thessalonians 4:16-17, as well as Paul in 2 Corinthians 12:4. The man child is caught up and appears before the throne of God.

To prove the man child and the 144,000 are the same, lets first establish that the 144,000 are clearly Jews, and their number is simply and literally stated in Revelation 7:1-8. There are 12,000 of them out of 12 tribes of Israel.

> And after these things I saw four angels standing on the four corners of the earth, holding the four winds of the earth, that the wind should not blow on the earth, nor on the sea, nor on any tree. And I saw another angel ascending from the east, having the seal of the living God: and he cried with a loud voice to the four angels, to whom it was given to hurt the earth and the sea, Saying, Hurt not the earth, neither the sea, nor the trees, till we have sealed the servants of our God in their foreheads. And I heard the number of them which were sealed: *and <u>there were</u> sealed an <u>hundred and forty and</u> four thousand of all the tribes of the children of Israel. Of the <u>tribe of Juda</u> were sealed twelve thousand. Of the <u>tribe of Reuben</u> were sealed twelve thousand. Of the <u>tribe of Gad</u> were sealed twelve thousand. Of the <u>tribe of Aser</u> were sealed twelve thousand. Of the <u>tribe of Nepthalim</u> were sealed twelve thousand. Of the <u>tribe of Manasses</u> were sealed twelve thousand. Of the <u>tribe of Simeon</u> were sealed twelve thousand. Of the <u>tribe of Levi</u> were sealed twelve thousand. Of the <u>tribe of Issachar</u> were sealed twelve thousand. Of the <u>tribe of Zabulon</u> were sealed twelve thousand. Of the <u>tribe of Joseph</u> were sealed twelve thousand. Of the <u>tribe of Benjamin</u> were sealed twelve thousand* (Rev. 7:1-8).

I have spoken to people who think they might be one of the 144,000, but we must be honest with Scripture and understand that the church, nor any denomination professing to be the church will make up this great company of saints. The 144,000 are "an hundred *and* forty *and* four thousand of all the tribes of the children of Israel" (Rev. 7:4).

There are three more times they are spoken of in Scripture in Revelation (9:4; 12:4-5; 14:1-5). Revelation 9:4 says the fifth and sixth trumpet judgment angels are told to hurt only those men which have not the seal of God (God's name) in their foreheads. We are told in Revelation 7:3 that this was done to the 144,000 Jewish Christians in order to protect them from the plaques. Revelation 12:4-5 calls them the man child, because they are Jews, meaning they are birthed from Israel. Israel is often referred to as a woman (Isa. 54:1-6; Jer. 3:1-14; Hos. 2:14-23). The sun, moon, and 12 stars spoken of in connection to the woman and the man child in Revelation 12:1-5 symbolizes Israel, as proved by Joseph's dream in Genesis 37:9-11.

The Jews are the only people in Scripture spoken of as going through travail in the last days (Isa. 66:7-8; Jer. 30: 6-9; Mic. 5:3; Zech. 12:10 – Zech. 13:1; Mat. 24:8; Mk. 13:8; Rev. 12:2-5), proving the woman and the man child to be Israel. There are also three classes of people referred to in Scripture; they are Jews, Gentiles, and the church (1 Cor. 10:32). The church is gone at Revelation 4:1, proving all things in Revelation 4 – Revelation 22 are after the church age (Rev. 2 – 3). So again, the man child cannot be any members of Gentiles or the church. Also, Gentiles are the ones persecuting Israel at the time of the middle of the Tribulation, so the man child cannot be Gentile. They are Jews.

Isaiah foretells Israel as bringing forth the man child (Isa. 66:7-8) before she is rescued and saved at the end of the Tribulation (Zech. 12:10 – Zech. 13:1; Rom. 11:25-29). Does Israel not bring forth the man child, who are proved to be Jewish (Rev. 7:1-8)? Of course she does! Who, if not the 144,000, does Israel bring forth before her deliverance and salvation that takes place at the Second Coming (Rev. 7:1-8; 14:1-5)? Which takes us forward to Revelation 14:1-5, where the 144,000 are mentioned specifically for the last time in Scripture.

> And I looked, and, lo, <u>a Lamb stood on the mount Sion</u>, and with him <u>an hundred forty *and* four thousand</u>, having his Father's name written in their foreheads. And I heard <u>a voice from heaven</u>, as the voice of many waters, and as the voice of a great thunder: and I heard the voice of harpers harping with their harps: And they sung as it were a new song <u>before the throne</u>, and <u>before the four beasts, and the elders</u>: and no man could learn that song but <u>the hundred *and* forty *and* four thousand</u>, which were redeemed <u>from the earth</u>. These are they which were not defiled with women; for they are virgins. These are they which follow the Lamb whithersoever he goeth. These were redeemed from among men, *being* the firstfruits unto God and to the Lamb. And in their mouth was found no guile: for they are without fault <u>before the throne of God</u> (Rev. 14:1-5).

The next mention of the 144,000, by the identifying number of "144,000," is when they are in heaven before the throne of God, who were redeemed from the earth. They are clearly in heaven, yet there was no mention of the Antichrist overtaking them, nor plaques, which they were sealed and protected from. There is also no mention at all of their death and destruction, so how did they get to heaven? The man child is delivered from earth and caught up to heaven right before the Great Tribulation, which is the last 3 ½ years of the Seven Year Tribulation, known as the greatest tribulation the earth as ever seen.

Daniel prophesies the deliverance of all born again Jews will happen just before the beginning of the great tribulation upon Israel (Dan. 12:1; Jer. 30:6-9; Mat. 24:15-22; Rev. 11:3; 12:13-17; 13:1-8). This happens 3 ½ years after the rapture of the church. John reveals to us that this company of saved Jews are the 144,000 and will be delivered by rapture (Rev. 12:5-6). Daniel says that all those among God's people will be delivered at that time whose names are written in the book of life. The number of the Jewish people written in the book of life is also discovered in Revelation 7:1-8 and Revelation 14:1-5.

> And at that time shall Michael stand up, the great prince which standeth for the children of thy people: and there shall be <u>a time of trouble, such as never was since there was a nation</u> *even* <u>to that same time</u>: and <u>at that time thy people shall be delivered, every one that shall be found written in the book</u> (Dan. 12:1).

As we have discovered from God's ways of delivering His people from His wrath, it is very often by rapture (Rev. 12:5). The 144,000 are the third of five exclusive fellowship of saints to be transported from the earth to go to heaven to live until the Second Coming takes place. We have two more raptures to go. The next two companies of saints will face death, though all are alive and well at the moment you are reading this. Unlike the 144,000, who will not die, the last two raptures will include a resurrection. All will be raptured up to heaven in their order and partake in the marriage supper of the Lamb (Rev. 19:1-10). That precedes the Second Coming and will be the last event in heaven before Jesus leads His army to take back the earth (Rev. 19:1- 21).

GLORIFIED AND ETERNAL BODY THE TRIBULATION SAINTS AT THE END OF THE TRIBULATION

There are a great number of people living today who will have a chance like no other. They will be left behind and will understand that they were not living righteous, God-centered lives, fully consecrated to Him in a life of holiness (Eph. 5:27; 2 Cor. 6:14 – 7:1; 1 Thess. 3:13 – 1 Thess. 4:17; Tit. 2:11-13). Some will understand quickly (Rev. 6:9-11). These people living today, unknowingly to themselves at this time, will be the great multitude of tribulation saints who are saved after the rapture of the church that happens a few weeks before the Seven Year Tribulation begins (proven in book 3).

Not all tribulation saints will be believers at the time of the rapture, but many will have the profession of a believer, but the possession of the unbeliever (Rev. 21:8). They will have a belief with no follow at the time of the trumpet sound. They will have been deceived into thinking they can be hearers of the Word only, and still be saved while living in their sin (James 1:22-25; 1 Cor. 6:9-10). I meet many in my life, and even after I tell them what the Bible says about their sin, they refuse to conform to the light of God (Rom. 12:1-2). I am confident I have spoken to many people who will wake up in the Tribulation and take their profession serious.

This company of believers will come to Christ in belief and full repentance to the point of not loving their lives unto death (Mat. 10:28-42; 12:11; 20:4). The first martyrs of that time are told to rest until the rest of them are killed (Rev. 6:9-11). They wait for the appropriate time of retribution that will take place after many more saints are martyred. They will all be raptured at the end of the days before the Second Coming and in time for the marriage supper (Rev. 7:9-17;

15:2-4; 20:4-6). This includes absolutely everyone in Christ who is killed throughout the entire seven years, being that time in between the rapture of the church and the end of the Tribulation, minus the two witnesses who will have their own rapture in time for the marriage supper (Rev. 19:1-10) and in time to come back with Christ (Joel 2:1-11; Zech. 14:5; Jude 1:14; Rev. 19:11-21). When Jesus comes back to earth at the Second Coming, all of heaven is emptied out, unless some angels stay behind for an unspoken purpose. But every human being will ride with Christ and take back the earth (Joel 2:1-11). No person will be merely a spirit and soul, though they certainly are able to ride a horse.

At this great time when even the angels come back to help take back the earth in righteousness, all human saints of God who have died or been raptured will have their resurrected body. No saint will be left in heaven without being resurrected. Just as the dead in Christ in heaven will come back to be reunited with their natural body to be changed and resurrected in immortality, thus the same experience will occur for those future saints who die for the name and sake of Christ in the soon coming Tribulation.

Did you know that God the Father will even be accompanying His Son, the saints, and the armies of heaven made up of the saints and the righteous angels? So when I say heaven will be emptied out at this time, I mean it! God the Father will be at the Second Coming as well (Dan. 7:9, 13-14, 22; Zech. 14:5; Tit. 2:13). At this time God the Father will come to help Jesus demolish and overcome the Antichrist kingdom (Dan. 7:21-22). He will then give the kingdom over to His Son and the saints (Dan. 7:13-14, 18, 27). Christ will be the King over all the earth and all the earth's kings, which will be the saints. Thus, the Lamb will be the Lion, and He will be, though He has always been, the King of all kings (Dan. 7:13-14, 27; Zech. 14:9; Mat. 25:31-46; Rev. 11:15; 20:1-10; 22:4-5)!

> And I saw <u>heaven opened</u>, and behold a white horse; and <u>he that sat upon him *was* called Faithful and True</u>, and <u>in righteousness he doth judge and make war</u>. His eyes *were* as a flame of fire, and on his head *were* <u>many crowns</u>; and he had a name written, that no man knew, but he himself. And he *was* clothed with a vesture dipped in blood: and <u>his name is called The Word of God. And the armies *which were* in heaven followed him upon white horses</u>, clothed in fine linen, white and clean. And out of his mouth goeth a sharp sword, that with it <u>he should smite the nations</u>: and <u>he shall rule them with a rod of iron</u>: and <u>he treadeth the winepress of the fierceness and wrath of Almighty God</u>. And he hath on *his* vesture and on his thigh a name written, <u>KING OF KINGS, AND LORD OF LORDS</u> (Rev. 19:11-16).

God the Father will then go back to heaven to remain living there for the first 1,000 years. Once Jesus and His saints have rid the earth of all rebellion (1 Cor. 15:24-28; Eph. 1:10), then the Father will dwell with man on earth forever. Rest assured, the Father will not be unseen by His saints for a thousand years, for the saints will then live in their mansions, built in the New Jerusalem (Jn. 14:1-3). The Holy City's foundations are still in heaven at that time (Rev. 21:9-27). If Jesus' resurrected body is an indicator of what the saints glorified bodies will be like, then the saints will travel at the speed of thought in order to rule the earth as kings and priests, for Christ did appear in a far off city at great speeds after His resurrection.

However the saints will travel, it will be speedily in order to go to and from heaven, and to rule the nations with a rod of iron with Jesus Christ (Ps. 2; Rev. 19:15), the Old Testament saints (Jer. 30:9; Ezek. 34:24; 37:24-25; Dan. 7:18, 27; Hos. 3:5; Mat. 8:11-12), the church saints (Mat. 19:28; Rom. 8:17; 1 Cor. 4:8; 6:2; 2 Tim. 2:12; Rev. 1:5-6; 2:26-27; 5:10; 22:4-5), the 144,000 (Rev. 12:5), and the tribulation saints (Rev. 20:4-6). "This honour have all His saints" (Ps. 149:6-9), including the two witnesses (Zech. 4:11-14; Rev. 11:3-12).

The tribulation saints will be, without exception, martyrs of the future tribulation, and not one will be martyred during the church age. All martyred saints during the church age will have already been resurrected and living in heaven in their glorified body seven years before the resurrection of the great multitude of tribulation saints. Most of these martyrs will be killed by the Antichrist, or the authority he gives to kill these saints (Rev. 7:14; 13:7; 14:12-13; 15:1-5; 20:1-4).

A smaller portion will be killed by the great whore of Revelation 17:6-7, which is a religious system dominating throughout the Revised Roman Empire in the first half of the Tribulation. This system will be overthrown and destroyed by the Antichrist and the 10 kings who have hated the whore! The Antichrist then sets up beast worship, which is where he declares himself to be God (Mat. 24:15; Rev. 17). Without proving this here, the great whore religious system will either be Catholicism, which has ruled the majority of the Old Roman Empire territory for the majority of the church age, or Islam, which also fits the biblical description and is taking over that territory even as you are reading this.

GLORIFIED AND ETERNAL BODY THE TWO WITNESSES AT THE END OF THE TRIBULATION

The rapture of the two witnesses is the last and final phase of the first resurrection, which began with the resurrection of Christ (Rev. 11:7-11). Some, if not most, have been taught that the ministry of the two witnesses will begin at the beginning of the Tribulation, or 70th Week of Daniel (Dan. 9:24-27). So the understanding is naturally that they are resurrected at the beginning of the Great Tribulation, or half way through the Seven Year Tribulation. I suppose I will need to prove the timing of their 1,260-day ministry in order to prove they are the last resurrection and rapture of the first resurrection. I'd love to do so and I'm always delighted to clear up inaccurate information and improve understanding in the realm of studying end-time prophecy. We'll get to that after some distinct facts are presented.

First, I'll introduce this as a rapture like Jesus', which is specific only to them. I love showing all the unique differences in all the raptures through time. Even in the first resurrection, there are different ways of going about the resurrections and changing of the bodies whether dead or alive, and raptures have some differences and some common features, though the end result is the same.

In Acts chapter 1, Jesus is giving the Great Commission again, then Scripture says:

> And when he had spoken these things, <u>while they beheld, he was taken up</u>; and <u>a cloud received him out of their sight. And while they looked stedfastly toward heaven as he went up</u> ... (Acts 1:9-10).

> And after three days and an half the Spirit of life from God entered into them, and they stood upon their feet; and great fear fell <u>upon them which saw them</u>. And they heard a great voice from heaven saying unto them, <u>Come up hither</u>. And <u>they ascended up to heaven in a cloud</u>; and <u>their enemies beheld them</u> (Rev. 11:11-12).

As you can see, both Jesus and the two witnesses will ascend fairly slowly to heaven in a cloud, which could very well be hiding the door, or portal, to heaven (Rev. 4:1; 19:11). They went, or will go, slow enough for all eyes in the area to watch them. There is no secret revelation or hidden meaning to this, it's just cool. The rapture of the church will be in a moment, in the twinkling of an eye. The Greek says *en* (GSN-<G1722>) *atomo* (GSN-<G823>), in an atom of time (1 Cor. 15:2), which is too fast to be seen.

The saints in heaven brought back to be resurrected and raptured are a part of the rapture of the church and seem to indicate the tribulation saints will be resurrected just as fast as those in heaven now. The 144,000 in the middle of the tribulation are alive on earth at their change and rapture, just like the rapture of the church, so it seems their transporting will happen in the blink of an eye as well.

It really will be an awesome sight to see these two great men of God, Enoch and Elijah, be raised from the dead and slowly rising toward the clouds as all their enemies shriek in terror. I'll be in heaven and I have no doubt, yet no proof, that I'll be able to see what's happening on earth. What's even more spectacular to think about is being part of the rapture of the church and seeing these two old saints in heaven for three and a half years, and in their preserved and natural bodies, before they begin their awe-inspiring mission on earth as witnesses for Christ (Rev. 11:3-12; Gen. 5:24; 2 Ki. 2; Ezek. 20:33-44; Zech. 4:11-14; Mal. 4:5-6; Heb. 11:5).

With that set up, it's time to prove the timing of their ministry, whether the first half, or the second half of the 7 Year Tribulation. All passages in both Daniel and Revelation speaking of forty-two months, 1,260 days, and three and one-half years always refer to the last half of Daniel's Seventieth Week. Revelation 11, which is where the two witnesses entire 3 ½ years has been summed up in the Book of Revelation says:

> But the court which is without the temple leave out, and measure it not; for it is given unto the Gentiles: and the holy city shall they tread under foot <u>forty *and* two months</u>. And I will give *power* unto my two witnesses, and they shall prophesy <u>a thousand two hundred *and* threescore days</u>, clothed in sackcloth (Rev. 11:2-3).

Besides being a reference to the last half of the Tribulation based upon the time given, it also directly speaks of the holy city, Jerusalem, being trodden down by the Gentiles, as well as the temple being given over to the Gentiles. As most dispensationalists know and understand, the Jewish people rebuild and have control of the temple and the Holy City during the first half of the Tribulation. This is accomplished because the Antichrist secures the Jews right to control their land and build their temple at the beginning of the seven years. He is actually the protector of Israel and her people by way of the covenant he has made with them over their enemies (Dan. 9:24-27).

The two witnesses are not making war with the Antichrist and defending Israel at the time when the Antichrist is acting as a friend to Israel. The two witnesses, Enoch and Elijah, will prophesy during the 1260 day period of time that the Antichrist rules dominant as a dictator and authoritarian over Israel. This is when the Holy City is trampled down by the Gentiles, and when Israel takes flight for her life into the wilderness for protection (Rev. 11:2-3; 12:6, 14; 13:5).

Malachi 4:5-6 proves that the time of their ministry is before the great and notable day of the Lord, which contrary to some beliefs, will begin at the coming of Christ and end at the renovation of the heavens and the earth (2 Pt. 3:10-13). It will be Jesus' day of rule on earth, not man's rule on earth which has been the case for 6,000 years. 2 Peter 3:10-13 speaks of the day of the Lord when the earth is renovated by fire. A thousand years is as a day to God, and so it is, the Day of the Lord is a thousand years, which is the Millennium Reign of Christ.

Many believe the Day of the Lord is the Tribulation era. But even then, Malachi 4:5-6 would mean Elijah, one of the two witnesses, would be coming back before the Tribulation begins. We must get a good understanding of doctrinal terms so all Scripture can then be harmonized. Understanding the simplicity of when the Day of the Lord is will easily place their ministry during the last three and one-half years of this church age, proving them to be the last of the resurrected and raptured saints in the first resurrection. It's time to get right with God and stay that way friends.

Here's a fun fact for you from an analytical researcher you have never heard before. Their ministry is 1,260 days, which ends the 7 Year Tribulation, which is when most believe the Second Coming will be. I used to believe this also. I thought it would be easy for the people on earth to figure out when the Second Advent of Christ would be, since all they would have to do is add 2,520 days (1,260 x's 2) after the rapture and the day would be known.

The problem with that is, there will be a small gap of time in between the rapture and the beginning of the Tribulation. There will also be a small gap between the end of the Tribulation and the Second Coming based upon the timing of the two witness' rapture. All references to the unknowing of the day and hour are all references to the Second Coming, which I dive deep into in the third book of the Millions Vanished series, *The Watcher's Guide*.

You see, the two witnesses will be resurrected and raptured to heaven in order to make the marriage supper of the Lamb (Rev. 19:1-10), which takes place before the Second Coming (Rev. 19:11-21). You don't think these two men will be making mad advances for the kingdom of God during the craziest time on earth and miss out on the feast do you? No way, Jose! They will make it up there without a rapture yo-yo effect. They won't ascend to the clouds just to come right back down. There will be no rapture or resurrection of any man at the Second Coming. No one dead or alive will be raptured at this point.

By this time, when Christ leaves heaven through the open door of Revelation 19:11, all raptures will have taken place and the first resurrection will be accomplished. It'll be time for the beginning of the next phase for man. His plan is to bring us back where He created us to be, before the fall of Adam (Gen. 3; Rom. 5:12-21). Rest assured though, there will be many people on earth who will be righteous, born again, holy, elect, sanctified, etc., yet not one of them will be changed or raptured at the Second Coming. Those in Christ on earth on that day will just go into the eternal earthly kingdom as natural people to be subjects of Christ and the raptured saints. These having part in the first resurrection will become rulers of the kingdom forever and ever (1 Cor. 6; Rev. 1:5; 5:10; 20:4-6; 22:4-5).

RAPTURES
CONDEMNED MAN
SOUL AND SPIRIT ONLY

Just as all (which are few) who are redeemed from sin at death go to heaven, all sinners and unbelievers (which is many) at death will go to the fires of hell for eternity. Everyone who has ever lived or been created as an angelic being or human being will be a part of one of two place, heaven or hell. Those in heaven will be able to freely leave and enter all parts of the universe, while those who have their portion in hell will be confined there forever as an eternal monument, showing eternal generations that rebellion against God does not pay (Isa. 66:22-24; Rev. 14:9-11; 20:11-15; 21:8).

For humans, this is on the condition of conformity and obedience to the Word of God with it's many conditions of eternal life (Jn. 3:15-19, 36; 4:14, 35-38; 5:24; 6:27, 37, 40, 44-45, 47, 50-51, 54-53, 58, 65; 10:27; 12:25; 17:2-3; Mat. 7:13-14; 18:8-9; 19:17; Mk. 10:28-30; Lk. 18:28-30; Rom. 1:5; 2:7; 5:21; 6:16-23; 8:1-13, 24; 2 Cor. 5:17; Gal. 6:7-8; 1 Tim. 6:12, 19; Tit. 1:2; 2:11-14; 3:7; Heb. 12:14-15; 1 Pet. 1:5, 9, 13; Jas. 1:12; 1 Jn. 2:24-25; 3:14-15; 5:11-20; Jude 1:20-24; Rev. 2:7, 10-11, 17, 26; 3:5, 12, 21).

The angels are not our main concern, but their destination is based on their continuous obedience to God. They were created righteous and must remain righteous, this is also what humans must do when they come to Christ to be redeemed (Mat. 5:48; 1 Tim. 5:20-22; 2 Tim. 2:19; 1 Pt. 1:13-17; 1 Jn. 3:1-3, 8-10; Rev. 2:5, 16; 3:3, 19; 21:7-8). However, there is a chance for us through repentance and faith in the only sacrifice for man, bringing redemption again (1 Jn. 1:9). There is no redemption for the angels. This mystery will be understood in time, but the Bible is only a primary source for the redemption and story of man, with few details concerning the existence of angels, yet enough details to unfold an amazing story.

Soul and Spirit Only
All Sinners and Unbelievers Who Will Ever Die and Go to Hell
All Souls in Hell Brought to Their Body to be Brought to Judgment

All sinners and unbelievers stand before God condemned. While on earth, all sinners and unbelievers have time to repent and be pure from their impurity, clean from their filth, innocent from their guilt, and holy from their sin. This life is only a short probationary period, a glimpse of time to repent and choose to follow Jesus. If the sinner and / or unbeliever dies in that condition, then they remain that way forever and will be transported to hell to await the judgment with the eternal sentence being eternal fire (Rev. 21:8; 22:11).

All souls in hell will be transported to their body for that appointed day of judgment (Rev. 20:11-15). All humans who physically die while in a state of spiritual death due to sin and trespasses against a holy God will be eternally dead in a conscious and immortal state in fire and tormented forever. Repent from your sins to a holy God and be free from the fate of this rapture of the soul to hell. To be free has never meant the penalty of sin can never be on the Christian's account, for the wages (what you are owed for something) of sin is death (Gen. 2:17; Ex. 32:33; Ezek. 18:4, 20, 24-26; Rom. 6:14-23; 8:1-13; Jas. 1:13-16). The ones set free from sin are now free to live obedient lives to Christ, completely conformed to His ways (Jn. 8:31-36; Rom. 12:1-2; 2 Cor. 6:14 – 2 Cor. 7:1; Tit. 2:11-14; 1 Pt. 1:13-17).

Natural Body
People Found to be Goats at the Judgment of Nations at the Second Coming

This story is discussed toward the end of chapter 5 and is called the Judgment of the Nations, where the sheep and goats are gathered from many nations by angels in order to be judged based on their treatment of the Jewish people (Mat. 25:31-46). The sheep are those who are declared innocent by Jesus. They enter the Millennial Reign and kingdom of heaven. The goats have been declared guilty by Jesus and are cast alive into hell fire. It appears as if their natural bodies will be changed to their immortal condition, because Scripture never says they are killed, as is the case with the Antichrist and his false prophet (Isa. 11:4; Dan. 7:11; 2 Thess. 2:8-9).

> Then shall he say also unto them on the left hand, <u>Depart from me, ye cursed, into everlasting fire</u>, prepared for the devil and his angels (Mat. 25:41).

> <u>And these shall go away into everlasting punishment</u>: but the righteous into life eternal (Mat. 25:46).

In the case of the goats, they appear to be raptured like the church and the 144,000, who are translated and changed to their immortal state without facing physical death, therefore have no resurrection, just a rapture. They have two raptures then, one from their places from which they are found on the earth by the holy angels, and another when they are transported straight into everlasting fire in the lower parts of the earth (Mat. 12:40; 25:41, 46; Eph. 4:8-10; cp. with Ps. 16:10; 63:9; Job 11:8; Dt. 32:22; Isa. 14:9 66:22-24; Prov. 9:18; 15:24; Ezek. 31:14-18; 32:18-24).

ETERNAL BODY
THE ANTICHRIST AND THE FALSE PROPHET

The rapture of the man of sin and his false prophet has been discussed at the end of chapter 5, but to elaborate further, they have no resurrection at the end of the Millennium (Rev. 20:11-15). When Christ destroys them they will be resurrected and cast alive into the lake of fire. They will not be resurrected at the end of the Millennial Reign. Their rapture is only when they are transported in their immortal state from earth, to the inner parts of the earth where the lake of fire is (Isa. 66:22-24; Eph. 4:8-10; Rev. 14:9-11).

Revelation 19:20 may appear as if they were not killed, but thrown alive into the lake of fire, meaning they simply did not die. That verse says:

> And the beast was taken, and with him the false prophet that wrought miracles before him, with which he deceived them that had received the mark of the beast, and them that worshipped his image. These <u>both were cast alive</u> into a lake of fire burning with brimstone (Rev. 19:20).

It reads like they will have to be resurrected at the end of the Millennial Reign because they have not been changed yet. Perhaps their natural bodies are burnt up in hell and their spirit bodies will have to be rejoined with their natural bodies, as all human beings will be resurrected and immortal.

This is simply not the intended meaning behind the passage in Revelation 19:20, "cast alive." Let's examine further.

Paul reveals the Antichrist will be consumed and destroyed, while Daniel reveals he will be slain and his body destroyed.

> For the mystery of iniquity doth already work: only he who now letteth *will let*, until he be taken out of the way. And then shall that Wicked be revealed, whom the Lord shall consume with the spirit of his mouth, and shall destroy with the brightness of his coming (2 Thess. 2:7-8).

> I beheld then because of the voice of the great words which the horn spake: I beheld *even* till the beast was slain, and his body destroyed, and given to the burning flame (Dan. 7:11).

The real meaning of Revelation 19:20 is that they will be killed, but immediately resurrected and cast into the fire of hell. This is what it means by saying they will be cast alive, because although other scriptures reveal their bodies will be killed, slain, consumed, and destroyed, only an eternal resurrection would make any sense for them to be cast alive into the fire. This is how the Antichrist and the False Prophet will be raptured. Just as the eternally resurrected righteous humans will be taken straight to heaven, in the same manner will these two men be resurrected and taken to the fires in hell.

What good is it to gain the whole world for a few years if you forfeit your own soul for eternity? If you want to gain the world, you must give your entire being to God. Then He will give you everything. This is the only way to exist, and by losing your own life, you will not be missing a thing. Instead, you will gain everything (Mat. 10:37-42). Whoever lives a life of self-gratification will lose it; whoever puts to death the sinful deeds of the body will gain it (Rom. 8:12-13; Gal. 5:16-26).

Eternal Body
Goats at the Judgment of Nations at the Second Coming Sent to Hell

We've spoken a couple times on this subject, so I guess I should've warned you when I gave that spoiler alert. The goats, those who mistreated the Jewish people during the Tribulation and will be declared guilty by Jesus, will be cast alive into hell's fires (Mat. 25:41, 46). Scripture seems to indicate they are transported to their eternal place in an immortal body, just like the rapture of the church before the beginning of the Tribulation, and as the 144,000 who are translated before the beginning of the Great Tribulation at the half way point of the 7 Year Tribulation. If this is true, then they will have no natural death or resurrection to immortality, though they will be changed to immortality as they are cast into hell.

If they are killed by capital punishment for their treatment of the Jewish people (Gen. 12:1-3), then their bodies will need to be buried and it will only be their soul and spirit that are cast into hell to await the final sentencing to the lake of fire (Rev. 20:11-15; 21:8; Isa. 66:22-24). The goats will then be raptured one more time, but instead of the traditional view of a rapture merely being from earth to heaven, they will be raptured from hell to the throne of God. Though, I do believe wording in Scripture leans toward the goats being cast body, soul and spirit into hell.

If the latter is true, the New Testament does teach the death penalty for certain transgressions (Rom. 13:1-7; 1 Tim. 1:8-10; Jas. 2:10-13; 4:11-12; 1 Pet. 2:13-15). Death penalty sins will even exist for natural people throughout the Millennium (Isa. 65:20). Both testaments list several sins that condemn the soul and obtain the eternal death penalty in the lake of fire if death or judgment comes and there has been no repentance (Jer. 23; Ezek. 3:18, 33; Mk. 7:20-23; Rom. 1:18-32; 1 Cor. 6:9-11; Gal. 5:19-21; Col. 3:5-10; 2 Pet. 2; Jude 1:3-19). Though the law of Moses has been abolished by Jesus when He made the new contract (Acts 15:5-29; Rom. 10:4; 2 Cor. 3:6-15; Gal. 3:19-25; 4:21-31; 5:1-5, 18; Eph. 2:15; Col. 2:14-17; Heb. 7:11-28; 8:6-13; 9:1-22; 10:1-18), the same sins it condemned are still condemned in New Testament scriptures, for all acts except breaking the Sabbath.

Eternal Body
Natural People Who Rebel With Satan at the End of the Millennium

Everyone who is left alive at the end of the 7 Year Tribulation who has not been judged and sentenced to hell at the Judgment of the Nations by Christ (Mat. 25:31-46) will be permitted to enter the kingdom of heaven, not to be mistaken with heaven itself. The kingdom of heaven here is the Millennial Reign ruled by Christ and His saints who had part in the first resurrection.

> And he shall set the sheep on his right hand, but the goats on the left. Then shall the King say unto them on his right hand, Come, ye blessed of my Father, <u>inherit the kingdom</u> prepared for you from the foundation of the world (Mat. 25:33-34).

That's why Scripture says, "Blessed *is* he that waiteth, and cometh to the thousand three hundred and five and thirty days" (Dan. 12:12). The next verse (Dan. 12:13) teaches us that saints will judge the world and rule forever under the Messiah (Dan. 2:44-45; 7:13-14, 18, 27; Lk. 22:30; 1 Cor. 6:2-4; 2 Tim. 2:12; Rev. 2:27; 5:10; 12:5; 20:4-6; 22:4-5). The natural man will enter the kingdom and be subjects who reproduce the human race to eternal generations (Gen. 1:26-28; 8:22; 9:12; Ps. 127:3; Isa. 9:6-7; 59:21; Dan. 2:44-45; 7:13-14, 27; Lk. 1:32-33; Rev. 11:15; 22:4-5).

> And I saw thrones, and they sat upon them, and judgment was given unto them: and *I saw* the souls of them that were beheaded for the witness of Jesus, and for the word of God, and which had not worshipped the beast, neither his image, neither had received *his* mark upon their foreheads, or in their hands; and they lived and reigned with Christ a thousand years. But the rest of the dead lived not again until the thousand years were finished. This *is* the first resurrection. Blessed and holy *is* he that hath part in the first resurrection: on such the second death hath no power, but they shall be priests of God and of Christ, and shall reign with him a thousand years (Rev. 20:4-6).

Following the prior passage of Revelation 20:4-6, we learn that all natural people, subjects of the kingdom, will be tempted at the end of the Millennium when Satan is released from his prison in the abyss (Rev. 20:7). He will be permitted one last time to form a rebellion against God with all the demons and fallen angels as well (Isa. 24:22). The Millennial Reign is still a time of testing for mankind. The ruling saints who have been part of the first resurrection have been proven and will not ever fall. Revelation says:

> And when the thousand years are expired, Satan shall be loosed out of his prison, And <u>shall go out to deceive the nations</u> which are in the four quarters of the earth, Gog and Magog, to gather them together to battle: <u>the number of whom *is* as the sand of the sea</u>. And they went up on the breadth of the earth, and compassed the camp of the saints about, and the beloved city: and <u>fire came down from God out

of heaven, and devoured them. 1And the devil that deceived them was cast into the lake of fire and brimstone, where the beast and the false prophet *are*, and shall be tormented day and night for ever and ever (Rev. 20:7-10).

The number of natural people who rebel against the rule of Jesus is an untold amount, a great multitude. Who knows how populated the earth will be after 1,000 years of repopulating it in a time when natural man will not die unless he commits a death penalty crime (Isa. 65:20).

I have often thought about the insanity of the holy angels who were under direct rule of the holy Trinity, yet still rebelled. They were in heaven witnessing the creation of the earth (Job 38:4-7). They had it all. They were also created in the likeness of God, for descriptions of them in Scripture reveal they have bodies that look like ours. They were also called the sons of God (Gen. 6:4; Job 1:6; 2:1; 38:4-7), though their sonship was by creation like Adam (Lk. 3:38), not by adoption like other redeemed humans (1 Jn. 3:1-3), or by begetting like Jesus alone (Jn. 3:15-21). They were able to be in the very presence of God, yet one third decided to rebel against His ways and His rule (Rev. 12:3-4).

How foolish these angels were, and still will be as they will fight against God three more times: once in the middle of the Tribulation (Rev. 12:7-12), next at the battle of Armageddon (Rev. 19:17-21; Isa. 24:22), and a final time at the end of the Millennial Reign before they are all cast into the lake of fire, prepared for all angelic beings after they rebelled the first time (Ezek. 28:11-18; Isa. 14:12-14; Mat. 25:41). But this is EXACTLY what happens with the natural people who rebel against God to fight against Jesus and the saints at the end of the Millennium!

How can one ponder or even begin to understand how man can be under perfect rule, and have strong bodies for the entire thousand-year reign, and still choose to fight against Him? What we know for certain is that there will be many waiting for their opportunity to rebel against their righteous government, and when Satan and his comrades give them the chance, they will take it.

These people will most likely be changed to their immortal body, not resurrected. Revelation 20:9 says, "They will go up on the breadth of the earth, and compass the camp of the saints about, and the beloved city of Jerusalem, when at that time fire will come down from God out of heaven, and <u>devoured them</u>." Like the goats during the Judgment of the Nations, it reads like they will be changed immediately to their immortal state when the fire devours them.

This is right before the Great White Throne Judgment happens (Rev. 20:11-15), and the fire devouring them may be the same fire that renovates the heavens and the earth, which will result in the New Heaven and New Earth (2 Pet. 3:10-13; Rev. 20:7-10; 21:1 – Rev. 22:5). If it is the same fire, then they will most likely be changed immediately and appear before the throne of God simultaneously with all damned souls in hell for the last judgment ever to take place, ridding the universe of loose rebels and enemies of God.

If the fire coming out of heaven to devour the rebel force is not the same as the fire that renovates the earth in 2 Peter 3:10-13, which I believe it is, then they will go to hell and then immediately be caught up before God for the Great White Throne Judgment, which would in consequence be a yo-yo effect. Either way, they will be transported rather quickly to destruction. What a horrible reality this will be for a people who have been born into an earth covered by the glorious reign of God the Son. I am not sure if the tribulation saints who enter the kingdom will be so unwise as to rebel, having lived through the Tribulation and seen the wrath of God, but that possibility exists, especially for those who were born into the 7 Year Tribulation and have no memory of that era.

Eternal Body
Those in Hell to be Judged at the Time of the Great White Throne Judgment

> And it shall come to pass in that day, *that* the LORD shall punish the host of the high ones *that are* on high, and the kings of the earth upon the earth. And they shall be gathered together, *as* prisoners are gathered in the pit, and shall be shut up in the prison, and <u>after many days shall they be visited</u> (Isa. 24:21-22).

"After many days shall they be visited" refers to the end of the thousand-year reign of Christ when God empties hell and delivers up the dead who will be judged and cast into the lake of fire (Rev. 20:11-15). This is their story, and it's not as the song goes: "This is my story, this is my song. Praising my Savior, all the day long."

> And I saw a great white throne, and him that sat on it, from whose face the earth and the heaven fled away; and there was found no place for them. And I saw the dead, small and great, stand before God; and the books were opened: and another book was opened, which is *the book* of life: and the dead were judged out of those things which were written in the books, according to their works. And the sea gave up the dead which were in it; and death and hell delivered up the dead which were in them: and they were judged every man according to their works. And death and hell were cast into

the lake of fire. This is the second death. And whosoever was not found written in the book of life was cast into the lake of fire (Rev. 20:11-15).

The beast and false prophet will remain in the lake of fire during the 1,000 years (Rev. 19:17-21; 20:10) and not be resurrected to stand judgment. This may be true as well for the goats, who were judged by God the Son right after the destruction of the Antichrist and false prophet. The rapture of the remaining untold number in hell will be when they are brought to their bodies on earth and in sea to be resurrected to immortality to stand before God, just to be transported back inside the earth where the lake of fire is forever. The lake of fire will have visibility in it for the people of earth to see for all eternity. This will be an eternal monument to show eternal beings that rebellion against God is not worth it and will not be tolerated (Isa. 66:22-24; Rev. 14:9-11). Then, death will finally be defeated, swallowing it up in victory forevermore.

Chapter 7

RAPTURE QUALIFICATIONS, HOW TO BE FOUND WORTHY

I often say there is no sin on the narrow path (Mat. 7:13-14). Think about whether that is true before you read on. Now, regardless of your initial answer, think about this: Is there any sin in Christ?

The Bible says Christ never sinned (2 Cor. 5:21; Heb. 4:15; 1 Pet. 2:22; 1 Jn. 3:5-7) and we are to be like Him (1 Pt. 2:20-21; 1 Jn. 2:3-6). I believe the Bible is the final authority (2 Tim. 3:16-17; 2 Pt. 1:19-21; Rev. 22:18-19). Now, is there any of Christ in sin? This has been the discussion through the ages of many who question the "dualism of God and the devil", but according to the Bible, the answer is, no. Satan had a beginning (Isa. 14:12-14; Ezek. 28:11-15; Jn. 1:14), and he also has an ending of his limited authority (Isa. 14:15; Ezek. 28:16-18; Rev. 20:1-10). God does not need a polar opposite to fulfill what He has purposed, but is using Satan's rebellion to test man to see who we will choose.

The Bible says the saints are in Christ (1 Thess. 4:16-17; 2 Cor. 5:17; 1 Cor. 15:23; Gal. 5:24), while the sinners are in sin (Mk. 7:21-23; Jn. 8:31-34; Rom. 1:29-32; 3:23; 8:1-13; 1 Cor. 6:9-11; Gal. 5:16-26; 1 Jn. 3:4; 5:15). So let's make sense of my questioning above with one more question, bring it full circle, and then prove it emphatically throughout this chapter. Can a person be "in Christ" and "in sin" simultaneously? No, this is an impossibility and the first lie the devil ever told man (Gen. 3:4). The righteous cannot be in sin and keep their righteous standing (Gen. 2:17; Ezek. 18:24-32). Even when the righteous sin, God will blot their names out of the Book of Life (Ex. 32:32-33; Ps. 69:20-28; Rev. 3:5; 22:18-19). There is no sin on the narrow road, just like there is no life on the broad path (Lk. 13:24-27).

There are many qualifications given in Scripture surrounding rapture verses that speak of the conditions to partaking in the rapture, therefore the first resurrection. These many qualifications can be summed up by two words, which will be unquestionably verified in the text below. To be raptured, one must be "in Christ." While the majority of Christians will agree with that condition, most do not understand the Bible meaning of being in Christ, for they believe a Christian will always sin, yet still be in Christ, therefore saved.

One of the leading pastors of Christendom has taught there is only one condition to being raptured, and that condition is to be alive. He referenced 1 Thessalonians 4:16-17 for this false teaching, which again says:

> For the Lord himself shall descend from heaven with a shout, with the voice of the archangel, and with the trump of God: and the dead <u>in Christ</u> shall rise first: <u>Then we which are alive *and* remain</u> shall be caught up together with them in the clouds, to meet the Lord in the air: and so shall we ever be with the Lord.

This tremendously influential pastor of the false teaching of unconditional eternal security speaks of all living, professing Christians, but that is not even the condition given from 1 Thessalonians 4:16-17.

The same conditions for going to heaven and receiving unforfeitable eternal life are the same for those at the end of their life and those alive at the end of the church age. In other words, there are not two sets of conditions for going to heaven; taken at death as opposed to being taken to heaven by the rapture event. All must be in Christ, whether dead or alive. I suppose the great confusion is people's understanding of what being "in Christ" means. Let's see what the Bible says.

> Therefore *if* any man *be* <u>in Christ,</u> *he is* a new creature: <u>old things are passed away</u>; behold, all things are become new. And all things *are* of God, who hath reconciled us to himself by Jesus Christ, and hath given to us the ministry of reconciliation; To wit, that God was in Christ, reconciling the world unto himself, not imputing their trespasses unto them; and hath committed unto us the word of reconciliation. Now then we are ambassadors for Christ, as though God did beseech *you* by us: we pray *you* in Christ's stead, be ye reconciled to God. For he hath made him *to be* sin for us, who knew no sin; that we might be made the righteousness of God in him (2 Cor. 5:17-21).

If you are in Christ, all things are passed away, that is all things of your sinful nature, your sinful spirit, and the power of sin, which is the old man, which according to the Dake Bible is nothing more nor less than the spirit, nature, and power of the devil working in men of disobedience (Jn. 8:44; Eph. 2:2; 2 Cor. 4:4; 1 Jn. 3:8; 5:18). Both outward and inward sin must pass away or one cannot claim to be in Christ. The theory that only outward transgressions are forgiven and one is still under control of the old man (the devil) is one of the most erroneous doctrines in Christendom (Rom. 6:6-23; 8:1-13; 2 Cor. 5:17-18; Eph. 4:24; 1 Jn. 5:18). The true Christian does not permit anything in his life which is ungodly and not Christ-like (Rom. 6:14-23; 8:1-13; Gal. 5:16-26), if they are reconciled to God (2 Cor. 5:18; Rom. 5:10; Eph. 2:14-18; Col. 1:20-21).

Even the word "if" is a red flag for those who believe there are no conditions in receiving salvation for those who are believers. Notice the conditional word at the beginning of the biblical definition of being "in Christ." "...<u>if</u> any man *be* <u>in Christ</u>, *he is* a new creature: <u>old things are passed away</u>; behold, all things are become new." This is to say any man can be in Christ, not a chosen few, but it is conditional. Any man who is in Christ has ceased from the old man, which is sin, the spirit, nature, and power of the devil working in men of disobedience (Jn. 8:44; Eph. 2:2; 2 Cor. 4:4; 1 Jn. 3:8; 5:18).

So if any man, even a man who has truly been forgiven of all his past sins (Jn. 5:14; 8:34; Rom. 3:25; 6:1-23; 8:12-13; Gal. 5:21; 2 Cor. 5:10), does decide to turn back to sin, even one (Ezek. 18:4, 20, 24-26; 33:12-13, 18; Rom. 6:16-23; 8:12-13; Heb. 10:26-29; Jas. 2:10-11; 5:19-20), then he is not in Christ until further repentance has been made (Mk. 6:12; Lk. 13:1-5; Acts 2:38; 3:19; Rom. 2:4-6; 2 Cor. 7:10; 1 Jn. 1:9; Rev. 2:5, 16, 22; 3:19).

Let me paint a simple, yet undeniably true picture. Repenting is an about face from Satan and sin, toward Jesus and righteousness. An "about face" is a military term that commands a soldier to do a half turn to face the polar opposite direction. There is no sin in Jesus, and no righteousness in Satan. The two are polar opposites. When a person repents with faith in Jesus, that person has just turned from Satan and sin, and toward Jesus and righteousness. If that person is tempted again by sin and from Satan, which they will be, then this is not sin as long as they keep their eyes on Jesus and their back to sin. If though, that person does sin, then it means they have turned from Jesus and now have their back to Him.

To be in Christ is quite contrary to being in sin, yet the popular belief in Christendom is all Christians are continually in both simultaneously. To be "in sin" or "in Christ" means to be in union with sin, or Christ. You can fall in sin and call yourself a Christian, this is the age of profession after all (Mat. 13:39-50), but falling in sin is a 180 degree turn with your back to Christ. You would then be in union with sin and death (Gen. 2:17; Ex. 32:33; Ezek. 18:4, 20, 24-26; 33:11-18; Rom. 6:23; 8:12-13; Jas. 1:13-16; Rev. 21:8). You profess Christ, yet be a Satanian, or a follower of Satan. Sinning is following Satan (Jn. 8:31, 44, 51; 1 Jn. 3:8-10).

Yes, this fact has been true every time I've fallen into sin's deceitfulness as well. Have I not ever sinned since first coming to Christ? Oh no, I had compromised to pornography's snare that lead to a long road of fighting my flesh to be free again. This never has to happen. Freedom in Christ means we are now able to live in obedience to God, conforming completely to His ways (Mat. 5:48; 2 Cor. 10:4-6). We never have to take our eyes off Jesus. If you do sin, repent and be saved from sin's penalty of death (Rom. 6:16-23; Gal. 4:19; Jas. 5:19-20; 1 Jn. 1:9; 2:1-6; Rev. 2:5, 16; 3:3, 19).

You simply cannot serve sin and righteousness (Jn. 8:31-36; 1 Jn. 1:5-7; 2:3-6; 3:8-10). The path that is narrow is facing Jesus. All living Christians on earth, that is to say all those in Christ, are on the narrow road, but have not actually walked through the narrow gate. This will only happen if found in Christ, not in sin, at physical death, or at the rapture of the church (Dan. 12:2; Mat. 7:13-14; 18:8-9; 19:28-29; Mk. 10:29-30; Lk. 18:29-30; Jn. 5:28-29; Rom. 2:7; 6:21-23; Gal. 6:7-8; 1 Tim. 1:16; 4:8; 6:12, 19; 1 Pet. 1:5, 9, 13; 3:7; 1 Jn. 2:25; Jude 1:20-24).

Until then, salvation is only a hope, even though we possess it now. That is, eternal salvation is only a hope (Rom. 8:20-25; 1 Thess. 5:8; 2 Thess. 2:16; 1 Pet. 1:5, 9, 13) for those in Christ, even though those in Christ have received initial salvation now in this time (Heb. 3:6; 6:11, 18-19; Tit. 1:2; 1 Pet. 1:3, 13). It means we must not grow weary, for in due time you will receive, if you don't faint, or stop running (1 Cor. 9:24-27; Gal. 6:7-9).

Some will say there is now no more condemnation for those who are in Christ Jesus... (Rom. 8:1). They are absolutely correct! But they fail to finish that verse, which says, "...who walk not after the flesh, but after the Spirit." Not walking after the flesh (Gal. 5:19-21) is a condition of remaining in Christ. Those who walk after the Spirit will remain in Christ (Gal. 5:22-26). The experience of Romans 7:7-24 was not Paul's condition at the time of the writing of Romans. It was a testimony of his life before he was in Christ, while he was living under the law.

I listened to the radio for a week with a well-known pastor teaching on Romans 8. He quoted the beginning of Romans 8:1 many times, but never finished the last half. The last half of Romans 8:1 is often left out from many translations.. He was of course teaching unconditional eternal security, or "Once Saved, Always, Saved." The famous pastor is so smart and I truly enjoy listening to him, but his salvation teachings are all over the place because of this deception. Salvation is for everyone (Jn. 3:16; 1 Tim. 2:4; 2 Pt. 3:9; Rev. 22:17), but it is not without conditions. We must remain in Christ. Let's look at John 15:1-6. Every believer in Christ is referred to by this illustration or it is meaningless.

> <u>I am the true vine</u>, and my Father is the husbandman. Every branch in me that beareth not fruit he taketh away: and every *branch* that beareth fruit, he purgeth it, that it may bring forth more fruit. Now ye are clean through the word which I have spoken unto you. <u>Abide in me</u>, and I in you. As the

branch cannot bear fruit of itself, except it abide in the vine; no more can ye, except ye abide in me. I am the vine, ye *are* the branches: He that abideth in me, and I in him, the same bringeth forth much fruit: for without me ye can do nothing. If a man abide not in me, he is cast forth as a branch, and is withered; and men gather them, and cast *them* into the fire, and they are burned (Jn. 15:1-6).

You see, being in Christ is the same as abiding in the Vine, or "Abide in Me" (Jn. 15:4). [Abide] Greek: *meno* (GSN-<G3306>), remain, continue, dwell, and abide. This is a command to remain in Christ. The reason is given here as not being able to bear fruit otherwise. If being in Christ was a guarantee of salvation without responsibility for one's own actions, or keeping the terms and agreements of the New Covenant, then such warnings are worthless from Christ.

I had a dream in February, 2016 where a young man was argumentative in tone and said:

> For by grace are ye saved through faith; and that not of yourselves: it is the gift of God: Not of works, lest any man should boast (Eph. 2:8-9)!

And I said, "YES, this is the first act of faith, the first step. For the just will live by faith. LIVE! A life of living it day by day, and if you don't live by faith until you die then you will go to hell."

It was pretty powerful. As I was replaying it in my head the next morning, I had some thoughts from these verses: Hebrews 10:38; James 1:22; 2:14, 17. These verses collectively say the just shall live by faith, but if any man draw back, my soul shall have no pleasure in him. What does it profit, my brethren, though a man say he hath faith, and have not works? Can faith save him? No, because faith without works is dead, vain, and worthless. But be ye doers of the word, and not hearers only, deceiving your own selves. Faith is the beginning of justification (Rom. 5:1; Eph. 2:8-9). Faith is also the continuation of justification (Heb. 10:38-39).

So what am I saying about the assurance of salvation? Can anyone know for sure if they are in right standing with God, therefore saved if they die in this moment? Absolutely! There are many Scriptures stating that any man (any person, man or woman) can be perfectly secure with the utmost confidence that they are a true, born again and righteously saved person.

> Whosoever believeth in Him should not perish, but have everlasting life ... hath everlasting life ... shall not come into condemnation; but is passed from death unto life (Jn. 3:15-16, 36; 5:24). There is now no condemnation to them which are in Christ Jesus... (Rom. 8:1). He shall be holden up: for God is able to make him stand (Rom. 14:4). You are sealed unto the day of redemption (Eph. 4:30). He which hath begun a good work in you will perform it until the day of Jesus Christ (Phil. 1:6). I am persuaded that He is able to keep that which I have committed unto Him against that day (2 Tim. 1:12). Who are kept by the power of God through faith unto salvation (1 Peter 1:5). Now unto Him that is able to keep you from falling, and to present you faultless before the presence of His glory (Jude 24).

More assurance of salvation verses are as follows: (Jn. 10:27-29; Rom. 5:8-9; 8:35-39; 1 Cor. 1:8-9; Eph. 1:4, 13; 1 Jn. 2:1-2; 3:2). Assurance of salvation is taught in Scripture, but conditions always abound throughout our covenant. You see, the New Covenant is still a covenant, and like all covenants, there have been conditions applied. This is just like our modern day terminology of a contract. Certain terms and conditions must be met in order for the contract to be honored by both parties. If one person dishonors the contract, then it has been broken, and made void.

Obedience is the basis of eternal security and the assurance of one's salvation. Obedience is not merely desired by God, though He knows man can never actually acquire enough control over self to meet His terms and agreements. No, how silly the entire language of the Bible is if there is no way to be found faithful in obedience. Christ alone makes you pure, then you must, with His continued ability and authority, keep yourself pure, or purify yourself by ceasing from sin and submitting totally in obedience (1 Tim. 5:20-22; 1 Jn. 3:1-10). Obedience is not desired for salvation, it is required (2 Thess. 1:7-10; Heb. 5:8-9; Rev. 14:12; 22:14-15). True security is through faith and obedience to God and grace, not disobedience and disgrace.

The qualifications to win this race are set forth in every rapture verse, passage, and chapter. Some say you can't be raptured unless you believe in the rapture. I used to see the possibility in that logic, but have since abandoned it by diving into Scripture, while leaving all my rationales and preconceived notions aside. It turns out that belief is important to be raptured, but this is to have the saving belief in Jesus, not a belief in the rapture, or even a good understanding of the subject at all. The only reason we are studying this is to have hope in the plan of God for man. The only requirement to be raptured, whether dead or alive, is to be "in Christ" (1 Thess. 4:16-17; 2 Cor. 5:17; 1 Cor. 15:23; Gal. 5:24).

This has been expressed in a few different ways in Scripture, and they can all be summed up by saying, "One must be in Christ." Simply looking these verses up will give any man the full truth God has conveyed on the subject of what it means to be in Christ. I found these points useful from the Dake Annotated Reference Bible:

1. Be "Christ's" (1 Cor. 15:23; Gal. 5:24).
2. Be "in Christ" (1 Thess. 4:16-17; 2 Cor. 5:17).
3. Be "blessed and holy" (Rev. 20:4-6; Heb. 12:14).
4. "Have done good" (Jn. 5:28-29).
5. Be in "the way, the truth, and the life" (Jn. 14:1-6).
6. Be "worthy" (Lk. 21:34-36).
7. Be in "the church" or "body of Christ" (Eph. 1:22-23; 5:27; 1 Cor. 12:13; Col. 1:18, 24).
8. Purify "himself, even as he is pure" (1 Jn. 3:2-3; 2 Cor. 7:1; 1 Tim. 5:20:22; Heb. 12:14).
9. Be "without spot or wrinkle ... and without blemish" (Eph. 5:27).
10. One must "walk in the light" (Col. 2:6-7; 1 Jn. 1:7).
11. One must "live and walk in the Spirit" (Gal. 5:16, 19-21)

Chapter 8

THE RAPTURE MOTIVATION

The rapture is a clear and present motivation for a life lived in constant holiness, void of sin. Let's establish once and for all the truth of the qualification to be raptured by simply looking at the most common and distinct rapture references. First, let's establish what some of the clear-cut Second Coming verses are and what some of the most common rapture verses are so the two won't get crossed. You will find that the most quoted rapture reference of all time is not in the rapture verses list. "Of that day and hour knoweth no man..." That is a Second Coming reference everywhere it is found (Mat. 24:36-44; 25:13; Mk. 13:32-37; Lk. 17:26-37).

There are two separate and distinct comings of the Lord. First, the rapture, when Jesus comes back FOR the saints (Lk. 21:34-36; Jn. 14:1-3; 1 Cor. 15:23, 51-54; 2 Cor. 5:1-8; Eph. 5:27; Phil. 3:11, 20-21; Col. 3:4; 1 Thess. 2:12; 19; 3:13; 4:13-17; 5:9, 23; 2 Thess. 2:1, 7; Titus 2:11-13; Jas. 5:7-8; 1 Pt. 5:4; 1 Jn. 2:28; 3:2; Rev. 4:1), separated by seven years when He comes to earth WITH the saints (Isa. 63:1-6; Dan. 2:44-45; 7:13-14, 18, 27; Joel 3; Zech. 14:1-5, 9, 16-21; Mat. 24:29-31; 25:31-46; 2 Thess. 1:7-10; 2:8; Titus 2:11-13; Jude 14-15; Rev. 1:7; 19:11-16; 20:1-3). So let's read the rapture verses and see with our own eyes the perfectly structured layout of the text, showing that holiness on our own part is required. We are made holy by Christ alone by His sacrifice that took away our past sins (Rom. 3:24-26), but after that, we are to remain in Him by keeping ourselves holy, which is free from sin (Mat. 5:48; Rom. 6:1-23; 8:1-13; Gal. 5:16-25; 2 Tim. 2:19; Tit. 2:11-13; 1 Pt. 1:13-17; 1 Jn.3:2-3; Rev. 2:5, 16; 3:19; 22:14-15).

> And take heed to yourselves, lest at any time your hearts be overcharged with surfeiting, and drunkenness, and cares of this life, and *so* that day come upon you unawares. For as a snare shall it come on all them that dwell on the face of the whole earth. Watch ye therefore, and pray always, that ye may be accounted worthy to escape all these things that shall come to pass, and to stand before the Son of man (Luke 21:34-36).

This is the first rapture reference in Scripture by Jesus. The command to remain holy is stated in the passage itself. For those who believe the rapture is far off, get lazy, stop watching, and slide back into the world (Jas. 4:4; 1 Jn. 2:15-17), they will not be able to escape the things (Tribulation – Lk. 21:25-28; Rev. 4 – Rev. 19) coming on the earth to stand in front of Him when He comes for His sinless church (Eph. 5:27; Tit. 2:11-13).

> Let not your heart be troubled: ye believe in God, believe also in me. In my Father's house are many mansions: if *it were* not *so*, I would have told you. I go to prepare a place for you. And if I go and prepare a place for you, I will come again, and receive you unto myself; that where I am, *there* ye may be also (John 14:1-3).

This is the first clear reference to the rapture that Jesus taught. In this chapter, Jesus says He is the way, the truth, and the life, and no one comes to the Father except by Him (vs. 6).

He then goes on to say you must keep His commandments if you love Him (vs. 15).

> He that hath my commandments, and keepeth them, he it is that loveth me: and he that loveth me shall be loved of my Father, and I will love him, and will manifest myself to him (Jn. 14:21). ...If a man love me, he will keep my words: and my Father will love him, and we will come unto him, and make our abode with him. He that loveth me not keepeth not my sayings... (Jn. 14:23-24).

Is there any sin allowed in keeping His sayings or commandments? If you sin, are you not following Satan (Jn. 8:31-51; 1 Jn. 3:8-10)? If you sin, you must repent again (1 Jn. 1:9; Rev. 2:5, 16; 3:19), or you will miss the rapture (Eph. 5:27; Tit. 2:11-13).

> But every man in his own order: Christ the firstfruits; afterward they that are Christ's at his coming (1 Cor. 15:23).

Then a few sentences later, in 1 Corinthians 15:34, many in the church of Corinth were commanded to awake to righteousness and stop sinning. Paul was writing to the Corinthians in order to address a few conditions and problems within the church. Chapter 5 – 6 of 1 Corinthians told these Christians about how their life and conduct should be free from the sins of their past because they will keep them from the kingdom of God (eternal life) (1 Cor. 5:1; 6:9-11). Another issue was concerning the resurrection, which is addressed in the 15th chapter (1 Cor. 15:12). Paul inserted another reminder to be sinless right in between a couple rapture references (1 Cor. 15:23, 51-54), and in the midst of the greatest resurrection chapter in the entire Bible. Shouldn't it be clear that being righteous is void of even one sin? Awake to righteousness and sin not, or you will not partake in the rapture of the church.

> Behold, I shew you a mystery; We shall not all sleep, but we shall all be changed, In a moment, in the twinkling of an eye, at the last trump: for the trumpet shall sound, and the dead shall be raised incorruptible, and we shall be changed. For this corruptible must put on incorruption, and this mortal *must* put on immortality. So when this corruptible shall have put on incorruption, and this mortal shall have put on immortality, then shall be brought to pass the saying that is written, Death is swallowed up in victory (1 Corinthians 15:51-54).

> For we know that if our earthly house of *this* tabernacle were dissolved, we have a building of God, an house not made with hands, eternal in the heavens. For in this we groan, earnestly desiring to be clothed upon with our house which is from heaven: If so be that being clothed we shall not be found naked. For we that are in *this* tabernacle do groan, being burdened: not for that we would be unclothed, but clothed upon, that mortality might be swallowed up of life. Now he that hath wrought us for the selfsame thing *is* God, who also hath given unto us the earnest of the Spirit. Therefore *we are* always confident, knowing that, whilst we are at home in the body, we are absent from the Lord: (For we walk by faith, not by sight:) We are confident, *I say*, and willing rather to be absent from the body, and to be present with the Lord (2 Corinthians 5:1-8).

And in this same chapter is the famous passage we have already spoken of that defines what it means to be in Christ (2 Cor. 5:17-21). The most famous rapture passage there is has told us that the requirement for the dead and living to partake in the rapture is to be in Christ (1 Thess. 4:16-17).

> That he might present it to himself a glorious church, not having spot, or wrinkle, or any such thing; but that it should be holy and without blemish (Ephesians 5:27).

This verse says it all! Could it be any more clear? The church, not the bride (as many misquote), that Jesus is coming back for will be spotless, holy, and without blemish. That does mean without sin. Jesus takes away all our sin, then it is up to us to remain this way by walking in obedience and free from sin (Jn. 15:1-14; 1 Jn. 3:1-10). Even a few verses back commands us to put off the old man, which is corrupt according to the deceitful lusts, and be renewed in the spirit of your mind, and that ye put on the new man, which after God is created in righteousness and true holiness (Eph. 4:22-24).

This is the same message as our poster verse for being in Christ by putting off the old man (2 Cor. 5:17). Again, in Ephesians 4:26, we are told to not sin. A reminder to these Ephesians was placed even closer to this rapture reference to remind them that the sexually immoral will not inherit the kingdom of God, so stop doing it and imitate God instead (Eph. 5:1-7).

> If by any means I might attain unto the resurrection of the dead (Philippians 3:11). For our conversation is in heaven; from whence also we look for the Saviour, the Lord Jesus Christ: Who shall change our vile body, that it may be fashioned like unto his glorious body, according to the working whereby he is able even to subdue all things unto himself (Philippians 3:20-21).

Paul expresses how he is not bodily perfect, that is by the glorification of the mortal body at the time of the rapture (vs. 12), but is telling them to be perfect in view of the rapture (vs. 15; Mat. 5:48; 2 Cor. 13:9, 11), and that he is still pressing toward the mark for the prize of the high calling of God in Christ Jesus (vs. 14). Yes, Paul was still pressing toward the prize, because he knew it could be lost, or forfeited (1 Cor. 9:24 – 10:12).

> When Christ, *who is* our life, shall appear, then shall ye also appear with him in glory (Colossians 3:4).

The following verses leave no room for doubt that in view of the rapture we are to put off the old man, like our definition of being "in Christ" tells us in 2 Corinthians 5:17.

> Mortify therefore your members which are upon the earth; fornication, uncleanness, inordinate affection, evil concupiscence, and covetousness, which is idolatry: For which things' sake the wrath of God cometh on the children of disobedience: In the which ye also walked some time, when ye lived in them. But now ye also put off all these; anger, wrath, malice, blasphemy, filthy communication out of your mouth. Lie not one to another, seeing that ye have put off the old man with his deeds; And have put on the new *man*, which is renewed in knowledge after the image of him that created him (Col. 3:5-10).

> For what *is* our hope, or joy, or crown of rejoicing? *Are* not even ye in the presence of our Lord Jesus Christ at his coming (1 Thess. 2:19).

In verse 10, Paul brings attention to his own example of how holy, justly, and unblameable he behaves. A Christian should be holy in reference to God, live justly in reference to man, and unblameable in reference to life and conduct before God and man. Paul teaches us to walk worthy of God, who has called us unto his kingdom and glory (vs. 12).

> To the end he may stablish your hearts unblameable in holiness before God, even our Father, at the coming of our Lord Jesus Christ with all his saints (1 Thess. 3:13).

Paul sent to know of the Thessalonians' faith, lest by some means the tempter have tempted them, and his labor be in vain (1 Thess. 3:5). Why would his labor be in vain if there was no possibility of Satan tempting Christians, causing them to fall and be lost? 1 Thessalonians 3:8 teaches, in view of the rapture (vs. 13), that we live only if we stand fast in Christ (Heb. 3:6, 12-14). We must remain in Him (Jn. 15:1-6; 2 Cor. 5:17). The rapture verses itself exclaims the truth of how righteous a person must be if they want to partake in this event (vs. 13). We must be unblameable in holiness before God. How much sin will God allow a person to have and stand before Him as holy?

> But I would not have you to be ignorant, brethren, concerning them which are asleep, that ye sorrow not, even as others which have no hope. For if we believe that Jesus died and rose again, even so them also which sleep in Jesus will God bring with him. For this we say unto you by the word of the Lord, that we which are alive *and* remain unto the coming of the Lord shall not prevent them which are asleep. For the Lord himself shall descend from heaven with a shout, with the voice of the archangel, and with the trump of God: and the dead in Christ shall rise first: Then we which are alive *and* remain shall be caught up together with them in the clouds, to meet the Lord in the air: and so shall we ever be with the Lord (1 Thess. 4:13-17).

Paul exhorts the Thessalonians again in chapter 4 by the Lord Jesus, that they should know how they ought to walk and to please God. He reminds them of the commandments he gave them by the Lord Jesus (vs. 2), and tells them the will of

God for them is their sanctification (vs. 3). Another time Paul has to tell Christians that ye should abstain from fornication (vs. 3; Eph. 5:3-7), and that every one of us should know how to possess our body in sanctification and honour (vs. 4), not in the lust of sexual desire, like the godless do which know not God (vs. 5). That no man should go and defraud his brother in any matter, because the Lord is the avenger of all such evil acts (vs. 6), and that God has not called us unto uncleanness, but unto holiness (vs. 7). All this in view of the rapture for those who are "in Christ" (vs. 13-17; 2 Cor. 5:1-8, 17).

> For God hath not appointed us to wrath, but to obtain salvation by our Lord Jesus Christ" (1 Thess. 5:9). And the very God of peace sanctify you wholly; and *I pray God* your whole spirit and soul and body be preserved blameless unto the coming of our Lord Jesus Christ (1 Thess. 5:23)

These two rapture references are in the same chapter, and verse 23 leaves no room for honest interpretation that a person must be blameless, which is only possible with God if a person is without sin. This verse also proves that the spirit and soul are not kept sinless while the body is always sinful until the resurrection. The truth is, if a righteous person sins in the body, then it also makes their spirit and soul sinful and in need of repentance again (Rev. 2:5, 16).

> Now we beseech you, brethren, by the coming of our Lord Jesus Christ, and *by* our gathering together unto him (2 Thess. 2:1). For the mystery of iniquity doth already work: only he who now letteth *will let*, until he be taken out of the way (2 Thess. 2:7).

These are also two rapture verses closely joined in one chapter. Let me just rewind a few verses to the previous chapter to show the severity of disobeying the gospel of Christ. These are from Second Coming passages, but God will not be faithful to those who disobey His gospel at one point in time, whether it's at the end of the church age, or seven years later.

> And to you who are troubled rest with us, when the Lord Jesus shall be revealed from heaven with his mighty angels, In flaming fire taking vengeance on them that know not God, and that obey not the gospel of our Lord Jesus Christ: Who shall be punished with everlasting destruction from the presence of the Lord, and from the glory of his power; When he shall come to be glorified in his saints, and to be admired in all them that believe (because our testimony among you was believed) in that day (2 Thess. 1:7-10).

> For the grace of God that bringeth salvation hath appeared to all men, Teaching us that, denying ungodliness and worldly lusts, we should live soberly, righteously, and godly, in this present world; Looking for that blessed hope, and the glorious appearing of the great God and our Saviour Jesus Christ (Titus 2:11-13).

This passage is by far one of my favorites. It proclaims the perfect standard to righteousness God has set, while doing so in view of the rapture and the Second Coming. Could there possibly be any doubt left that sin, even a little so-called "unknown" sin, will be tolerated on a person's account at the coming of Jesus for the church? How much sin is in sober living, righteous living, and godly living? It is certain, we must not be found in sin; we must be and remain in Christ.

> Be patient therefore, brethren, unto the coming of the Lord. Behold, the husbandman waiteth for the precious fruit of the earth, and hath long patience for it, until he receive the early

and latter rain. Be ye also patient; stablish your hearts: for the coming of the Lord draweth nigh (James 5:7-8).

Chapter 5 of James has its time element in the last days (vs. 3). Within the first six verses deals with the sins of wicked, rich men: heaping together treasures on earth (vs. 3; Mat. 6:19-21; Lk. 12:15-21), defrauding laborers (vs. 4; Lev. 19:13; Dt. 24:14-15; Jer. 22:13; Mal. 3:5), living in pleasure at the expense of those defrauded (vs. 5; Mat. 23:14), living in wantonness or sensual appetites to the uttermost (vs. 5; Rom. 13:13; 1 Tim. 5:11; 2 Pet. 2:18), nourishing the heart, or living in luxury and pride (vs. 5), condemning the just, or perverting the judgment of the poor (vs. 6; Jas. 2:1-10), and killing the just to multiply their own riches (vs. 6; 1 Ki. 21). The warning is for these wicked, rich men to fear God's judgment.

After that, we have a reference to the coming of the Lord, which is about the rapture, when the Lord will come in the air to receive the saints to Himself (vs. 7-8; Lk. 21:34-36; Jn. 14:1-3; 1 Cor. 15:23, 51-54; 2 Cor. 5:1-8; Eph. 5:27; Phil. 3:11, 20-21; Col. 3:4 ; 1 Thess. 2:19; 3:13; 4:13-17; 5:9, 23; 2 Thess. 2:1, 7; Titus 2:11-13; Jas. 5:7-8; 1 Pt. 5:4 ; 1 Jn. 2:28; 3:2; Rev. 4:1). Directly after that the brethren, Christians, are told to grudge not one against another lest we be condemned. Even sinning Christians are told that the judge standeth before the door.

Verse 12 gives another warning that the saved can be condemned. James 5:19-20 says it is possible for Christians to err from the truth and become unconverted, needing to repent to be saved again from death, and if he does, then his sins will be forgiven and hidden. These clear warnings are all surrounding a rapture verse, making it a plain and simple truth if one is honest with the human language. The truth is that sin will condemn all without respecter of person (2 Sam. 14:14; 2 Chr. 19:6; Acts 10:34; Rom. 2:11; Gal. 2:6; Eph. 6:9; Col. 3:25; 1 Pt. 1:17). If one wishes to partake in the coming of the Lord for the saints, then they must walk worthy (Lk. 21:34-36).

> And when the chief Shepherd shall appear, ye shall receive a crown of glory that fadeth not away (1 Pet. 5:4).

In view of the rapture, when the chief Shepherd will appear to take the righteous to heaven and give them a crown (1 Cor. 3:14-5; 2 Tim. 4:8; Rev. 2:10; 4:4), let the younger submit to the elder (1 Pt. 5:5), all submit to one another (1 Pt. 5:5), be clothed with humility (1 Pt. 5:5), humble yourselves to God (1 Pt. 5:6), cast all your care upon God (1 Pt. 5:7), be sober (1 Pt. 5:8), be vigilant (1 Pt. 5:8), and resist Satan in the faith (1 Pt. 5:9). Don't all these conditions sound like there is no room for error to be accepted and receive a crown (Jas. 5:19-20)?

Our crown can be taken away, for only the overcomer will receive a crown of life (Rev. 3:11). Those who are faithful unto death, or the rapture, are the overcomers. But take heart, for even those who are wicked their entire lives have the grace from God to repent at death and be declared an overcomer (Ezek. 18:24-26; Lk. 23:43).

> Behold, I come quickly: hold that fast which thou hast, that no man take thy crown (Rev. 3:11).

> And now, little children, abide in him; that, when he shall appear, we may have confidence, and not be ashamed before him at his coming (1 Jn. 2:28).

The Rapture Motivation

By simply understanding simple rules of interpretation and laws of implication, one can safely conclude that one will not have confidence of being in Christ and will be ashamed when He comes if one does not abide in Him. That person will be left behind. Abiding in Him is the exact same as remaining, or continuing in Christ (Jn. 15:1-10). Keeping the commandments is the sole assurance of continuance abiding (Jn. 15:10). Abiding is the stipulation of fruit-bearing (Jn. 15:4, 7). If one does not abide, he is cut off and destroyed like a branch (Jn. 15:6).

Two sided sticks are not thrown in a fire immediately after they separate from their life source. Life remains for a while, but one day the Gardner will gather up all dead sticks and burn them. Be a one sided stick, because it means you are attached to the life source.

Everyone who makes a Christian profession ought to walk as Christ did, and He walked without sin (1 Pet. 2:21; 1 Jn. 2:6; 3:1-10; 4:17). To be in Christ means that one is a new creature, the old man has passed away, and the affections and lusts of the flesh have been crucified (2 Cor. 5:17; Gal. 5:16-26; Rom. 8:12-13; Col. 3:5-10). This does not mean there is no temptation (2 Cor. 10:1-6; Jas. 1:13-16; 4:4-8; 1 Pt. 5:5-9), it means there is overcoming in victory (1 Cor. 9:24-27; Rev. 2:7, 11, 17, 26; 3:5, 12, 21).

Philippians 3 has three rapture verses (vs. 11, 20-21). To be found in Him at His coming is one of the purposes of abiding in Christ. To this end Paul says in Philippians 3 that he has counted all loss for Christ and made every known sanctification, or commitment to be found free of sin, or he would be rejected with the sinners (1 Cor. 9:24-27). This is the example of Israel for the Christian, even after Calvary (1 Cor. 10:1-12). "Let us therefore fear, lest, a promise being left us of entering into his rest (Heb. 4:1). Paul is saying we (Christians - holy brethren, Heb. 3:1, 6, 12-14) fear, lest we come short of eternal life. The promise here is clearly eternal life (Heb. 4:14; 9:15; 1 Jn. 2:25).

> And this is the promise that he hath promised us, *even* eternal life (1 Jn. 2:25).

> Beloved, now are we the sons of God, and it doth not yet appear what we shall be: but we know that, when he shall appear, we shall be like him; for we shall see him as he is (1 John 3:2).

This is a beautiful rapture verse. For it reminds us that those who abide in Him (1 Jn. 2:6, 28) will be like Jesus when He comes for us. This is referring to His glorified, immortal and incorruptible body that we will receive for eternity, if we continue in Him and not in sin.

The next verse tells us that every man that has this hope in him purifies himself, just like He is pure, and Jesus is sinless (1 Jn. 3:3, 5-7). The only hope of the rapture is to purify one's self even as Christ is pure (1 Jn. 1:7-9; 2:6; 3:3, 5-10; 5:1-4, 18). The rapture is an incentive and a constant motivation for holiness now, for how you leave this earth is how you remain for eternity (Rev. 22:11). There is no mystery to wondering who is righteous and who is not, for all who commit sin are of the devil, while all who do righteousness are children of God (1 Jn. 1:5-7; 2:29; 3:8-10). Only children of God have the hope of being raptured in the first resurrection (1 Jn. 3:2).

> After this I looked, and, behold, a door *was* opened in heaven: and the first voice which I heard *was* as it were of a trumpet talking with me; which said, Come up hither, and I will shew thee things which must be hereafter (Rev. 4:1).

The Rapture Motivation

This is the place in Revelation where the rapture happens. Revelation 1:19 is the key of the book that tells us Revelation is divided in three main sections: the things that John has seen as Christ was speaking to him in chapter 1, the things which are, which are the messages to the seven local churches in Asia Minor that also include the entire church age since it is a prophecy (1:3), and the things which shall be hereafter, that is the things after the church age found in Revelation 4 – Revelation 22.

Revelation 4:1 begins with "After this," and ends with "I will show you the things which must be hereafter," that is, after the church age. By this indicator, we must view the revealing of the rapture in Revelation 4:1 by the conditions laid out in the church age of Revelation 2 – Revelation 3. This could be a long and exhausted synopsis of the seven letters to the churches that represent present conditions found throughout the entire church age, but I'm going to sum it up quickly with the confidence that both chapters can be easily read and understood if the language is taken at face value. Only the over comer is promised heaven and eternal life (Rev. 2:7, 11, 17, 26; 3:5, 12, 21). Repentance is mandatory of all backsliders (sinning saints) (Rev. 2:5, 16, 21-22; 3:3, 19), or they will be removed (2:5), judged (2:16), and rejected (3:15-16).

CONCLUSION

Thinking first about yourself is normally a bad thing, but salvation is something only you can control for yourself. Two people in a falling plane both need oxygen, while one is passed out and the one awake is you. To help someone else, you must first be in a position of safety. You have become an expert in this subject. Most importantly, you understand what it takes to be a part of this event. Now, go and make disciples!

I'm so excited for the journey you've decided to go on. This is only the beginning folks! The greatest experience of your life is about to begin and never end! All your life you've been told no one knows the day or the hour. You'll be awestruck at how much you can actually know from Scripture, and how much God has intended you to understand from the beginning. The enemy wants us ignorant, not God! Make sure to get book three, *The Watcher's Guide*, and learn how close we are!

ABOUT THE AUTHOR

BRIAN LAKINS was ingrained into the Christian faith as a young child…then seeking his own ways for a season, the prodigal returned to Jesus with a God-given passion to write and speak to Christians and seekers to inspire them to live holy in an unholy world. He earned his degree in Biblical studies from Liberty University.

Wisdom was gained in the trenches of life, and the passion for Brian to address deep questions of faith beyond surface teachings was produced. Through years of personal study, the original *Millions Vanished* vision was birthed in 2005.

If you desire an in-depth study tool to discover truths from Genesis through Revelation surrounding the topics of the Raptures and Resurrections, then this book series is for you! You can contact Brian on his website:

www.millionsvanished.com

FOR FURTHER CONTACT

Website and Contact:
www.MillionsVanished.com
1thes4.16@gmail.com
https://www.facebook.com/brianplakins/
https://twitter.com/BrianLakins

OTHER BOOKS:

The Millions Vanished Series
Unveiling Raptures and Resurrections (Part 1)
7 Rapture Views (Part 2)
The Watcher's Guide (Part 3)
Signs of His Coming (Part 4)
Billions Left Behind (Part 5)

The Obedient Christian Series
My Road to the Path (Part 1)
Eternal Laws From God and Christian Warnings (Part 2)
Eternal Security's Evidence, Conditional Salvation's Verdict (Part 3)
The Billions Who Lost Salvation From Genesis Through Revelation (Part 4)
Tough Christian Questions, Tough Biblical Answers (Part 5)
The Lost Pillars of Conditional Salvation (Part 6)

www.ingramcontent.com/pod-product-compliance
Lightning Source LLC
LaVergne TN
LVHW051055080426
835508LV00019B/1890